POETRY OF
THE SECOND
WORLD
WAR

POETRY OF THE SECOND WORLD WAR

An International Anthology

EDITED WITH AN INTRODUCTION BY

DESMOND GRAHAM

Chatto & Windus

LONDON

First published in Great Britain 1995

1 3 5 7 9 10 8 6 4 2

Introduction and selection © Desmond Graham 1995
Desmond Graham has asserted his right under
the Copyright, Designs and Patent Act, 1988
to be identified as the author of this work.

Published in 1995 by
Chatto & Windus Limited
Random House, 20 Vauxhall Bridge Road,
London SW1V 2SA

Random House Australia (Pty) Limited
20 Alfred Street, Milsons Point, Sydney
New South Wales 2061, Australia

Random House New Zealand Limited
18 Poland Road, Glenfield
Auckland 10, New Zealand

Random House South Africa (Pty) Limited
PO Box 337, Bergvlei, South Africa

Random House UK Limited Reg. No. 954009

A CIP Catalogue record for this book
is available from the British Library.

ISBN 0 7011 6299 6

Designed by Humphrey Stone
Printed and bound in Great Britain by
Clays Ltd, St Ives plc

CONTENTS

III

'Boswell by my bed, Tolstoy on my table'

[vi]

IV

'Wounded no doubt and pale from battle'

V

'At night and in the wind and the rain'

VI

'Speechless you testify against us'

VII
'I am twenty-four led to slaughter I survived'

[xi]

VIII

'For dreams are licensed as they never were'

IX
'War is no longer declared but continued'

INTRODUCTION

The Second World War and Auschwitz have often been said to have silenced the poet, to have gone beyond words; to be too big to encompass, too terrible to find expression for: the war could not, above all, be expressed in poetry, that celebrating art from, that musical manner of speech, that making of beautiful things.

Time has shown, or rather, the poets have shown, quite the opposite to be the case. The need to break silence, to give witness, to relieve memory, to lament, cry out and question, has placed the Second World War in the centre of much of the poetry written during it and afterwards. The scale of the task has meant that it has needed time; though some did write contemporaneously, even in the most terrible circumstances. But poetry, with its artifice, its traditions of ways of saying and making fictions, has proved a positive aid to reaching towards the experience of the war.

The poems of that experience are gathered in this anthology. What emerges is a poetry capable of conveying the vast and terrible sweep of the war. A poetry in which human responses and experiences echo each other across boundaries of culture and state. Reading all these poems in English it is sometimes a surprise to find that some are translations, some not. At the same time details and nuances, the points of view from the different cultures, languages and poets, point back to the diversity and the scale of what took place. It is this immensity and variety of the war which the anthology sets out to convey. The experience, across time and people, of its course.

The poems were written both at the time and later, in almost equal numbers: I have made no distinction, though some are given dates by their poets and these are included. I have, however, generally limited myself to poems by those who were adult before the war's close. So much has been written of the war by the following generations, to have included poems by them would have needed another volume. I have also limited myself to poems which already exist in translation: one minute's thought would be enough to understand that to do otherwise would open the whole anthology up to an impossible task. I have sought help from poets, scholars and translators and have brought into being a few translations – in particular, of Baczyński, Poland's main 'war poet' – but this book is a gathering and not a monument. Some cultures are represented more thoroughly than others and the largest single selection is of poems originally in English; but from Australia, New Zealand and Canada as well as from America and Britain. With an impossible task, a 'world' anthology of a 'world' war's poetry, I can make no claim to being inclusive: within my chosen parameters, however, I have tried to select with authority, to aim at breadth and range and to bring the poems together so that they can speak.

The broad history of what had happened in literature throughout Europe, and pretty well world-wide, meant that poetry itself proved fairly ready for the task of writing of war. This may, of course, be putting cart before horse in a simple way. But for the writer from the 1920s on, poetry was already no longer wholly identified with beauty, the aesthetic, and with song, whether simple or epic. New potentialities of expressiveness had become normal to the writing of it; poets had turned to new, more open and variable forms; and, above all, there was a move – continuing through to this day – to bring poetry closer and closer to speech.

National traditions and language traditions met this 'modernizing' at different points and times, had different traditional strengths to offer the poet. In Japanese, for example, while the great literary impact of Europe came in the nineteenth century, it was only post-war, directly in response to the experience of the war, that the thorough-going 'modernizing' of poetry took place. Throughout Eastern Europe, a post-war move away from literary language coincided with the development of censorship and the police states of Stalinism: hence directness and statement combined naturally with allegory and obliquity. In Germany, many poets felt the language itself had to be re-made, started afresh to avoid the contamination of the Nazi past – Günter Eich's poem 'Inventory', included here, is a famous instance of this. Other poets, like Miklós Radnóti, in the midst of it, made their poetry out of the very conflict between their art and war:

Is there a land still, tell me, where this verse form has meaning?
Without putting in the accents, just groping line after line,
I write this poem here, in the dark, just as I live,
Half blind like a caterpillar inching my way across paper;
Torches, books – the *Lager* guards took everything . . .

There is no one 'international' phenomenon of poetry this century any more than there was one 'Second World War'; but a poetry which is more flexible and responsive to its subject matter, less distinctly 'poetic', more free and colloquial, is essentially more open to translation. In the 1940s, still, translations read very much like translations. By the start of the 1970s, translation practice had caught up with what had been going on in poetry: the translation had to be as readable as the poems in English which were themselves more colloquial, less literary. The emphasis within translation thus shifted towards the reader. This did mean sacrifices – the more elaborate poems could be left untranslated; effectiveness could overtake faithfulness – but this emphasis upon the reader meant that translation could become a form of currency rather than a paying of tribute. It also opened up the practice of translation to poets who would not previously have ventured upon it. Through collaboration or expert assistance, poets could work on poems from languages which alone they could not tackle; literatures less frequently translated became available. Through the 1970s and 1980s poems in translation became a thriving, even a central part of the life of 'English' poetry. Part of what was revealed, dotted about in anthologies, dominating or momentarily appearing in collections, was a poetry of the war, so extensive and compelling it overturns all those generalizations about the lack of Second War poetry.

This anthology begins and ends chronologically. It starts with pre-war intimations: sensed by Miklós Radnóti in a mountain garden in Hungary in 1936; by Osip Mandelshtam, in 1937, a year before his own death in Siberia, as he contemplates the misfortune of a birth date 'eighteen-ninety something'; by Charles Reznikoff, also a Jewish poet, on the seemingly safe west coast of America, receiving a letter which brings him to realize he may not be 'with Noah and the animals,/warm and comfortable in the ark' but with those to be drowned. It ends with the 'Aftermath' when, in the words of the Austrian Ingeborg Bachmann, 'War is no longer declared/but continued.'

Between these extremes is a broad onward sweep, each section carrying a descriptive title taken from one of the poems within it: *'By greatcoat, cartridge belt and helmet held together'* – conscription, military life, life in the Forces; *'Boswell by my bed, Tolstoy on my table'* – responses from the edge, places not immediately in the thick of it, people still managing within the Blitz, people feeling they are on the war's verge; *'Wounded no doubt and pale from battle'* – the battlefields, in Europe, North Africa and Asia, on land, at sea, in the air; *'At night and in the wind and the rain'* – the civilians caught up as refugees, under occupation, resisting, in forced labour, suffering the raids at Hiroshima; *'Speechless, you testify against us'* – the genocide of the Holocaust; *'I am twenty-four led to slaughter I survived'* – the meaning of being a survivor; *'For dreams are licensed as they never were'* – liberation, victory, recovery and continuation.

Each section is self-contained; as much as any aspect of the war could be said to have been so. Inevitably poems could take their place in one section or another, but their placing has never been without thought. At times within sections there is a certain chronological and experiential development but for the most part poems are arranged by theme and juxtaposition: sometimes aimed at contrast, sometimes harmony.

The anthology is a communal effort, with poems from about twenty countries and by a hundred and thirty poets. A number of the poets are central, however, among them: Brecht, the commentating voice of the 1930s, of exile, of a German under threat of death from his own country, his poems only really brought to light and made available in the 1970s; Stevie Smith, a commentator from London of equally acute intelligence; Różewicz, a survivor from the Polish resistance, writing a spare, painful poetry which reclaims a minimal humanity so as to resist the final triumph of war's nihilism; Pilinsky, a Hungarian, witness to the Camps and starvation of 1945; Sutzkever, a Yiddish poet, actually writing from the Vilna Ghetto during the war's progress, joining the Jewish resistance and surviving; Nelly Sachs, German, Jewish and a Psalmist of the Holocaust; Rachel Korn, another Holocaust survivor, writing in Yiddish in Canada; Primo Levi, the Italian Jewish writer famous for his prose works on Auschwitz and survival; Sankichi Toge who survived Hiroshima long enough to write of it and Tamiki Hara who survived and wrote of it, only to commit suicide at the confirmation of the symptoms of 'atom disease'.

Others left their witness before they were killed during the war: Radnóti, a well-established Hungarian Jewish poet before the war, turning to literally Classical form – the Eclogue – in order to counter barbarism with the 'civilization' which defined its evil, writing poems of Forced Labour which were found in his pocket when his corpse was disinterred at a roadside; 'Two children from Terezin' whose poems remain anonymous; Baczyński, a brilliant young poet killed in the Warsaw Uprising; Keith Douglas, probably the finest British poet of the war, killed in Normandy after having written poems as a tank officer from El Alamein on.

In Britain, in particular, there is a myth that the Second World War produced no 'war poetry', no battle poetry like that of the First. Here, the German poets Huchel and Bobrowski can be heard, as soldiers, alongside their erstwhile adversaries, the Russian poets Vinokurov and Slutsky: the Japanese poets Kaoru Maruyama, Nobuo Ayukawa and Ei Yamaguchi alongside James Dickey, John Ciardi and Howard Nemerov from America. Alan Ross, writing post-war, brings us the war at sea. From air bases in America, with little first-hand experience of action, Randall Jarrell writes of the Air Crew's war. From the wide range of Australian writing of the war, John Quinn and Eric Rolls write as soldiers in the Middle East and New Guinea; Donald Campbell as airman, and C. D. Griffin as a prisoner of war to the Japanese in the infamous Changi camp.

Almost a by-product of the anthology is that poems 'from the margin' (as Roy Fuller put it) reveal their true weight within the context of what they were on the edge of. Poems by Scovell, Blunden, Elizabeth Bishop or Seferis resonate so much more ominously within their context here. Similarly, the little known 'The Edge of the War' by William Montgomerie, written from Fife Ness, with its glimpsed submarines, suddenly appearing planes, gossip and intrusions of death, can take its place as a defining poem of war's edges. For too long, the 'poems of wartime' of British writing have sunk under the weight of numbers, surrounded by others on similar themes; their subtle, well-judged understanding of war's threats and insidious ways lost within inappropriate claims that they are 'war poems' like those of the 1914–18 war.

For what was the centre and what was the edge could be quite unclear. Anna Akhmatova from Leningrad wrote in sympathy for Londoners during the 1940 Blitz. Within three years she had written of Leningrad's suffering, while herself in Tashkent. Centre and margin, perhaps, could be clear to those whose experience was of war at its most terrible. Yet even at this point, there could be, so very rarely, a denial of war's absoluteness. Luba Krugman Gurdus, saved at one Polish collection point for a death camp, because an SS guard remembered her from art college in Berlin pre-war, lived on in hiding, within inches of the murderers' grasp, to write down poems for her dead child, killed by diphtheria: the extent of war's savagery, finding its way through virus and neglect, through heartbreak and loss as well as through weaponry.

I compiled this anthology so that such poems could be heard. Before making my acknowledgements, a quick word on the kinds of poem I have not included: French poetry suffers a little here; there was a great deal of poetry from the Resistance but of its nature it was coded and often the chosen code was literary subterfuge. Poems from Char and Aragon and Jean-Jouve are included. In isolated translations, however, the relevant poetry rarely reads well. Similarly, the crucial mass of Russian 'patriotic poetry', does not read well enough out of context. Tvardovsky's 'Tyorkin' (in an extract), however, is here. Translation problems limited my ability to draw on the immense work of Josef Leftwich (Isaac Rosenberg's childhood friend): his translations from Yiddish are, for the most part, tragically outmoded. Hundreds of poems from the war which deserve recognition could not find place because the war itself had been traced at too oblique an angle: Seifert, for example, writing wonderfully from memory, so often transposes war into a key of autobiographical rumination; T. S. Eliot, in the *Four Quartets*, makes from the London Blitz his Dantesque encounters. This anthology is not of 'poems from the war', or 'the best poems' connected with it; everything written during its course bears its mark in some way. This is an anthology of poems where the experience of the war is apparent and central: an anthology revealing the war through the poets' words.

For that reason, my saddest, necessary, omission is of poets who did not leave poems directly on the war but who were killed by it. They, in a sense, are the truest war poets of all. Because all our witness comes from survivors, however temporary or painful their survival, I will end with an account of Ohrenstein, a young Jewish poet living in Prague and publishing under a non-Jewish pseudonym, 'Jiri Orten'. In 1941, crossing the road to buy cigarettes, he was struck by a speeding German car. The first hospital to which he was taken refused him admission because he was Jewish. He died in the second.

I have included a brief biographical note on each poet, together with some help for further reading. The specific sources for the poems can be found in the list of Acknowledgements.

I would like to thank all those who have helped with this book. It has been ten years in the making, so there are more than I can list here. I must first stress, with especial force, the customary caveat that none of those mentioned is responsible for any error or shortcoming in my text. I may have consulted scholars on a single point or picked through their lengthy advice for what suited my immediate need. First, I would like to thank the British Academy for their assistance with a Research Grant; the School of English and the Research Committee of the University of Newcastle upon Tyne for grants towards travel and clerical assistance; Professor Bruce Bennett and the staff of the English Department at the Australian Defence Forces Academy, for their hospitality and help. Next are those who have helped or advised me in gathering material: Neil Astley, Petr Bilek, Dr Daniel Brint, Dr Joasia Burzyńska, Dr Adrian Caesar, Dr Małgorzata Czermińska, Jeff Doyle, John Drew, Gyozo Ferencz, Alan Gould, Janos Gyurgyak, Iain Halliday, Keiko Harada, Professor Martin Hilsky, Petr Holman, Miroslav Holub, Professor Roman Kalisz, Dr Wojtek and Ola Kubinsky, Professor Tomasz P. Krzeszowski, Kunos Laszlo, Graham McGregor, Adam Nadasdy, Dr James Naughton, Ewald Osers, Geoff Page, Professor Norbert Platz, Dr Dickie Sokolow, Piotr Somer, Professor Jon Stallworthy, Irumi Tytler, Zdenek Urbanek, Bob Webb, Dick Wilcocks, Professor Jacek Wisniewski, Anna Zukowska-Wilcocks. Finally, I would like to thank Neil Hairsine for administrative help and very much more; Professor R. S. White and Jane Whiteley for sustaining insights; Gordon and Wilma Meade for creative support throughout; Catharine Carver for her example; Carol Rumens for help at a crucial time; and Sara Holloway of Chatto for all her help through the final stages. To Trude Schwab, for sharing the making of it in every way, I would dedicate the book. It belongs, though, to the poets who made it, and their living memory.

Newcastle upon Tyne 1994

I

---

*'I lived on this earth
in an age . . .'*

BERTOLT BRECHT

from *A German War Primer*

(1936–1938)

When the leaders speak of peace
The common folk know
That war is coming.

When the leaders curse war
The mobilisation order is already written out.

• • •

It is night
The married couples
Go to their beds. The young women
Will bear orphans.

• • •

Those at the top say: peace and war
Are of different substance.
But their peace and their war
Are like wind and storm.

War grows out of their peace
Like a son out of a mother
He bears
Her terrible features.

Their war kills
Whatever their peace
Has left over.

• • •

On the wall was chalked:
They want war.
The man who wrote it
Has already fallen.

translated by H.R. Hays and Lee Baxenball

[3]

MIKLÓS RADNÓTI

A Mountain Garden

Summer has fallen asleep, it drones, and a grey veil
  Is drawn across the bright face of the day;
  A shadow vaults a bush, so my dog growls,
  His hackles bristling, and then runs away.

Shedding its petals one by one, a late flower stands
  Naked and half-alive; I hear the sound
  Of a withered apricot-bough crack overhead
  To sink of its own weight slowly to the ground.

O, and the garden too prepares for sleep, its fruit
  Proffered to the heavy season of the dead.
  It is getting dark. Late too, a golden bee
  Is flying a death-circle around my head.

And as for you, young man, what mode of death awaits you?
  Will a shot hum like a beetle toward your heart,
  Or a loud bomb rend the earth so that your body
  Falls limb from limb, your young flesh torn apart?

In sleep the garden breathes; I question it in vain;
  Though still unanswered I repeat it all.
  The noonday sun still flows in the ripe fruit
  Touched by the twilight chill of the dew fall.

Istenbegy (a Buda mountain), 1936
translated by Clive Wilmer and George Gömöri

OSIP MANDELSHTAM

Aortas Fill with Blood

Aortas fill with blood.
A murmur resounds through the ranks:

– I was born in '94,
I was born in '92 . . .
And, clutching the worn-out year of my birth,
Herded wholesale with the herd,
I whisper through anaemic lips:
I was born in the night of January the second and third
In the unreliable year
Of eighteen-ninety something or other,
And the centuries surround me with fire.

1937
translated by James Greene

MIGUEL HERNANDEZ

War

Old age in the towns.
The heart without an owner.
Love without any object.
Grass, dust, crow.
And the young ones?

In the coffins.

The tree alone and dry.
Woman like a stick
of widowhood across the bed.
Hatred there is no cure for.
And the young ones?

In the coffins.

translated by Hardie St. Martin

Hast Du dich verirrt?

My child, my child, watch how he goes,
The man in Party coloured clothes.

LOUIS MACNEICE

The Sunlight on the Garden

The sunlight on the garden
Hardens and grows cold,
We cannot cage the minute
Within its nets of gold,
When all is told
We cannot beg for pardon.

Our freedom as free lances
Advances towards its end;
The earth compels, upon it
Sonnets and birds descend;
And soon, my friend,
We shall have no time for dances.

The sky was good for flying
Defying the church bells
And every evil iron
Siren and what it tells:
The earth compels,
We are dying, Egypt, dying

And not expecting pardon,
Hardened in heart anew,
But glad to have sat under
Thunder and rain with you,
And grateful too
For sunlight on the garden.

1938

MORDECAI GEBIRTIG

Our Town Is Burning

Our town is burning, brothers, burning,
Our poor little town is burning.
Angry winds are fanning higher
The leaping tongues of flame and fire,
The evil winds are roaring!
Our whole town burns!

And you stand looking on with folded arms,
And shake your heads.
You stand looking on, with folded arms
While the fire spreads!

Our town is burning, brothers, burning,
Our poor little town is burning.
Tongues of flame are leaping,
The fire through our town goes sweeping,
Through roofs and windows pouring.
All around us burns.

And you stand looking on with folded arms,
And shake your heads.
You stand looking on with folded arms
While the fire spreads!

Our town is burning, brothers, burning.
Any moment the fire may
Sweep the whole of our town away,
And leave only ashes, black and grey,
Like after a battle, where dead walls stand,
Broken and ruined in a desolate land.

And you stand looking on with folded arms,
And shake your heads.
You stand looking on with folded arms
While the fire spreads!

Our town is burning, brothers, burning.
All now depends on you.
Our only help is what you do.
You can still put out the fire
With your blood, if you desire.

Don't look on with folded arms.
And shake your heads.
Don't look on with folded arms
While the fire spreads!

1938
translated by Joseph Leftwich

MARINA TSVETAYEVA

from *Poems to Czechoslovakia*

They took   quickly, they took   hugely,
  took the mountains and their entrails.
They took our coal, and took our steel
  from us, lead they took also and crystal.

They took the sugar, and they took the clover
  they took the North and took the West.
They took the hive, and took the haystack
  they took the South from us, and took the East.

Vary   they took and Tatras   they took,
  they took the near at hand and far away.
But   worse than taking paradise on earth from us
  they won the battle for our native land.

Bullets they took from us, they took our rifles
   minerals they took, and comrades too:
But while our mouths have spittle in them
   The whole country   is still armed.

translated by Elaine Feinstein

VLADIMIR HOLAN

Horoscope

Early evening.... Cemetery.... And the wind sharp as
bone splinters on a butcher's block.
Rust shakes its model out of tortured form.
And above it all, above the tears of shame,
the star has almost decided to confess
why we understand simplicity only when the heart breaks,
and we are suddenly ourselves, alone and fateless.

translated by Jarmila and Ian Milner

GEORGE SEFERIS

The Last Day

The day was cloudy. No one could come to a decision;
a light wind was blowing. 'Not a north-easter, the sirocco,'
   someone said.
A few slender cypress nailed to the slope and the sea,
grey with shining pools, beyond.
The soldiers presented arms as it began to drizzle.
'Not a north-easter, the sirocco,' was the only decision
   heard.
And yet we knew that by the following dawn

[9]

nothing would be left to us, neither the woman drinking
    sleep at our side
nor the memory that we were once men,
nothing at all by the following dawn.

'This wind reminds me of spring,' said my friend
as she walked beside me gazing into the distance, 'the
    spring
that came suddenly in winter by the closed-in sea.
So unexpected. So many years have gone. How are we going
    to die?'

A funeral march meandered through the thin rain.
How does a man die? Strange no one's thought about it.
And for those who thought about it, it was like a
    recollection from old chronicles
from the time of the Crusades or the battle of Salamis.
Yet death is something that happens: how does a man die?
Yet each of us earns his death, his own death, which belongs
    to no one else
and this game is life.
The light was sinking over the clouded day, no one decided
    anything.
The following dawn nothing would be left to us, everything
    surrendered, even our hands,
and our women slaves at the springheads and our children
in the granaries.

My friend, walking beside me was singing a disjointed song:
'In spring, in summer slaves . . .'
One recalled old teachers who'd left us orphans.
A couple passed, talking:
'I'm sick of the dusk, let's go home,
let's go home and turn on the light.'

Athens, February 1939
translated by Edmund Keeley and Peter Sherrard

W. H. AUDEN

September 1, 1939

I sit in one of the dives
On Fifty-Second Street
Uncertain and afraid
As the clever hopes expire
Of a low dishonest decade:
Waves of anger and fear
Circulate over the bright
And darkened lands of the earth,
Obsessing our private lives;
The unmentionable odour of death
Offends the September night.

Accurate scholarship can
Unearth the whole offence
From Luther until now
That has driven a culture mad,
Find what occurred at Linz,
What huge imago made
A psychopathic god:
I and the public know
What all schoolchildren learn,
Those to whom evil is done
Do evil in return.

Exiled Thucydides knew
All that a speech can say
About Democracy,
And what dictators do,
The elderly rubbish they talk
To an apathetic grave;
Analysed all in his book,
The enlightenment driven away,
The habit-forming pain,
Mismanagement and grief:
We must suffer them all again.

Into this neutral air
Where blind skyscrapers use
Their full height to proclaim
The strength of Collective Man,
Each language pours its vain
Competitive excuse:
But who can live for long
In an euphoric dream;
Out of the mirror they stare,
Imperialism's face
And the international wrong.

Faces along the bar
Cling to their average day:
The lights must never go out,
The music must always play,
All the conventions conspire
To make this fort assume
The furniture of home;
Lest we should see where we are,
Lost in a haunted wood,
Children afraid of the night
Who have never been happy or good.

The windiest militant trash
Important Persons shout
Is not so crude as our wish:
What mad Nijinsky wrote
About Diaghilev
Is true of the normal heart;
For the error bred in the bone
Of each woman and each man
Craves what it cannot have,
Not universal love
But to be loved alone.

From the conservative dark
Into the ethical life
The dense commuters come,
Repeating their morning vow;

'I *will* be true to the wife,
I'll concentrate more on my work,'
And helpless governors wake
To resume their compulsory game:
Who can release them now,
Who can reach the deaf,
Who can speak for the dumb?

All I have is a voice
To undo the folded lie,
The romantic lie in the brain
Of the sensual man-in-the-street
And the lie of Authority
Whose buildings grope the sky:
There is no such thing as the State
And no one exists alone;
Hunger allows no choice
To the citizen or the police;
We must love one another or die.

Defenceless under the night
Our world in stupor lies;
Yet, dotted everywhere,
Ironic points of light
Flash out wherever the Just
Exchange their messages:
May I, composed like them
Of Eros and of dust,
Beleaguered by the same
Negation and despair,
Show an affirming flame.

Great Babel Gives Birth

When her time was come she withdrew into her innermost chamber and surrounded herself with doctors and soothsayers.

There was whispering. Solemn men went into the house with grave faces and came out with anxious faces that were pale. And the price of white make-up doubled in the beauty shops.

In the street the people gathered and stood from morning till night with empty stomachs.

The first sound that was heard was like a mighty fart in the rafters, followed by a mighty cry of PEACE!, whereupon the stink became greater.

Immediately after that, blood spurted up in a thin watery jet. And now came further sounds in unceasing succession, each more terrible than the last.

Great Babel vomited and it sounded like FREEDOM! and coughed and it sounded like JUSTICE! and farted again and it sounded like PROSPERITY! And wrapped in a bloody sheet a squalling brat was carried on to the balcony and shown to the people with ringing of bells, and it was WAR.

And it had a thousand fathers.

translated by John Willett

BERTOLT BRECHT

The God of War

I saw the old god of war stand in a bog between chasm and rockface.

He smelled of free beer and carbolic and showed his testicles to adolescents, for he had been rejuvenated by several professors. In a hoarse wolfish voice he declared his love for everything young. Nearby stood a pregnant woman, trembling.

And without shame he talked on and presented himself as
a great one for order. And he described how everywhere he
put barns in order, by emptying them.

And as one throws crumbs to sparrows, he fed poor people
with crusts of bread which he had taken away from poor
people.

His voice was now loud, now soft, but always hoarse.

In a loud voice he spoke of great times to come, and in a
soft voice he taught the women how to cook crows and sea-
gulls. Meanwhile his back was unquiet, and he kept looking
round, as though afraid of being stabbed.

And every five minutes he assured his public that he would
take up very little of their time.

translated by Michael Hamburger

CHARLES REZNIKOFF

The Letter

I have heard of this destruction –
it is in our books.
I have read of these rains and floods,
but now I have only to go to the window
and see it.

I was always with Noah and the animals,
warm and comfortable in the ark,
and now –
is it possible? –
am I to drown
in the cold flood
with the wicked,
among the animals that have crawled upon the rocks and hills
in vain?

I walk slowly in the sunshine watching
the trees and flowers,
smelling a pungent weed, noting a bird's
two notes.

TADEUSZ RÓŻEWICZ

A Tree

Happy were
the poets of old
the world like a tree
they like a child

What shall I hang
upon the branch of a tree
which has suffered
a rain of steel

Happy were
the poets of old
around the tree
they danced like a child

What shall I hang
upon the branch of a tree
which is burnt
and never will sing

Happy were
the poets of old
beneath the oak
they sang like a child

But our tree
creaked in the night
with the weight
of a corpse despised

translated by Adam Czerniawski

MIKLÓS RADNÓTI

Fragment

I lived on this earth in an age
When man fell so low he killed with pleasure
And willingly, not merely under orders.
His life entangled, trapped, in wild obsession,
He trusted false gods, raving in delusion.

I lived on this earth in an age
That esteemed informers, in an age whose heroes
Were the murderer, the bandit and the traitor.
And such as were silent – or just slow to applaud –
Were shunned, as if plague-stricken, and abhorred.

I lived on this earth in an age
When any who spoke out would run for it –
Forced to lie low and gnaw their fists in shame.
The folk went mad and, drunk on blood, filth, hate,
Could only grin at their own hideous fate.

I lived on this earth in an age
When a curse would be the mother of a child
And women were glad if their unborn miscarried.
The living – with poison seething on his plate –
Would envy the grave-dweller the worms eat.

. . . .
. . . .

I lived on this earth in an age
When poets too were silent: waiting in hope
For the great Prophet to rise and speak again –
Since no-one could give voice to a fit curse
But Isaiah himself, scholar of terrible words.

19 May 1944
translated by Clive Wilmer and George Gömöri

[17]

II

'By greatcoat, cartridge belt and
helmet held together'

SORLEY MACLEAN

from *Poems to Eimhir*

The innocent and the beautiful
have no enemy but time.

W.B.YEATS

I thought I understood from you
that these lines were exact and true,
nor did I think that I would find
their falsehood bitter in my mind.

But that plausible epigram
proved itself another dream
when on that Monday I saw with dread
the steel helmet on your golden head.

translated by Iain Crichton Smith

RANDALL JARRELL

A Lullaby

For wars his life and half a world away
The soldier sells his family and days.
He learns to fight for freedom and the State;
He sleeps with seven men within six feet.

He picks up matches and he cleans out plates;
Is lied to like a child, cursed like a beast.
They crop his head, his dog tags ring like sheep
As his stiff limbs shift wearily to sleep.

Recalled in dreams or letters, else forgot,
His life is smothered like a grave, with dirt;
And his dull torment mottles like a fly's
The lying amber of the histories.

DOUGLAS STEWART

from *Sonnets To the Unknown Soldier*

We did not bury him deep enough: break up the monument,
Open the tomb, strip off the flags and the flowers
And let us look at him plainly, naked Man.
Greet him with silence since all the speeches were lies,
Clothe him in fresh khaki, hand him a rifle
And turn him loose to wander the city streets
Where eyes so quickly innured to death's accoutrement
Will hardly spare him a glance, equipped to die for us.

'You see that fellow with the grin, one eye on the girls,
The other on the pub, his uniform shabby already?
Well, don't let him hear us, but he's the Unknown Soldier,
They just let him out, they say he lives for ever.
They put him away with flowers and flags and forget him,
But he always comes when they want him. He does the fighting.'

1941

HENRY REED

Naming of Parts

Today we have the naming of parts. Yesterday,
We had daily cleaning. And tomorrow morning,
We shall have what to do after firing. But today,
Today we have naming of parts. Japonica
Glistens like coral in all of the neighbouring gardens,
And today we have the naming of parts.

This is the lower sling swivel. And this
Is the upper sling swivel, whose use you will see of,
When you are given your slings. And this is the piling swivel,
Which in your case you have not got. The branches
Hold in the gardens their silent, eloquent gestures,
Which in our case we have not got.

[22]

This is the safety catch, which is always released
With an easy flick of the thumb. And please do not let me
See anyone using his finger. You can do it quite easy
If you have any strength in your thumb. The blossoms
Are fragile and motionless, never letting anyone see
Any of them using their finger.

And this you can see is the bolt. The purpose of this
Is to open the breech, as you see. We can slide it
Rapidly backwards and forwards: we call this
Easing the spring. And rapidly backwards and forwards
The early bees are assaulting and fumbling the flowers;
They call it easing the Spring.

They call it easing the Spring: it is perfectly easy
If you have any strength in your thumb: Like the bolt,
And the breech, and the cocking-piece, and the point of balance,
Which in our case we have not got, and the almond-blossom
Silent in all of the gardens, the bees going backwards and forwards,
For today we have the naming of parts.

ROY FULLER

Waiting to be Drafted

It might be any evening of spring;
The air is level, twilight in a moment
Will walk behind us and his shadow
    Fall cold across our day.

The usual trees surround an empty field
And evergreens and gravel frame the house;
Primroses lie like tickets on the ground;
    The mauve island floats on grey.

My senses are too sharp for what the mind
Presents them. In this common scene reside
Small elements with power to agitate
      And move me like a play.

I have watched a young stray dog with an affection
Of the eyes, and seen it peer from the encrusted
Lids, like a man, before it ran towards me,
      Unreasonably gay.

And watched it gnawing at a scrap of leather
In its hunger, and afterwards lying down,
Its ineffectual paws against its cracks
      Of eyes, as though to pray.

Pity and love one instant and the next
Disgust, and constantly the sense of time
Retreating, leaving events like traps: I feel
      This always, most today.

My comrades are in the house, their bodies are
At the mercy of time, their minds are nothing but yearning.
From windows where they lie, as from quiet water,
      The light is taken away.

ALUN LEWIS

All Day It Has Rained . . .

All day it has rained, and we on the edge of the moors
Have sprawled in our bell-tents, moody and dull as boors,
Groundsheets and blankets spread on the muddy ground.
And from the first great wakening we have found
No refuge from the skirmishing fine rain
And the wind that made the canvas heave and flap
And the taut wet guy-ropes ravel out and snap.
All day the rain has glided, wave and mist and dream,
Drenching the gorse and heather, a gossamer stream

Too light to stir the acorns that suddenly
Snatched from their cups by the wild south-westerly
Pattered against the tent and our upturned dreaming faces.
And we stretched out, unbuttoning our braces,
Smoking a Woodbine, darning dirty socks,
Reading the Sunday papers – I saw a fox
And mentioned it in the note I scribbled home;
And we talked of girls, and dropping bombs on Rome,
And thought of the quiet dead and the loud celebrities
Exhorting us to slaughter, and the herded refugees;
– Yet thought softly, morosely of them, and as indifferently
As of ourselves or those whom we
For years have loved, and will again
Tomorrow maybe love; but now it is the rain
Possesses us entirely, the twilight and the rain.

And I can remember nothing dearer or more to my heart
Than the children I watched in the woods on Saturday
Shaking down burning chestnuts for the schoolyard's merry play,
Or the shaggy patient dog who followed me
By Sheet and Steep and up the wooded scree
To the Shoulder o' Mutton where Edward Thomas brooded long
On death and beauty – till a bullet stopped his song.

ALAN ROSS

Pilot Station, Harwich

Landmarks of sorts there always were,
Flamborough Head, Immingham, Southwold –
Sea-marks as well, the buoys
Marking the channel where E-boats,
Engines idling, waited for us, all contacts
Muffled. But they were mere signposts,
Not aspects of arrival –

No, the real landmark that made
The pulse quicken, coming up on deck

On a summer morning, was the black
And white pagoda of the Trinity House
Pilot Station, exotic to us as Konorak
Or Madurai. Anchoring there,
We could look down from above
At the launches swishing up the estuary
With signals and mail, Wrens at the helm
In bell-bottoms, their lovely hair flying.
It was the nearest we ever got to love.

DENIS GLOVER

Leaving for Overseas

They make an end at last, binding their friends
With words awkward as names on trees.
Water devours the land, the wave
Mocking every mountain-top of home.

A ship's wake heals slowly, like a wound.

Daily they watch horizon's saucer-rim
Slide tilting, where the whale
Takes his gigantic solitary bath. At night
Before the stars' silver tremendous stare
They button up a coat or turn to cards.

Swung on the arc of war towards older islands
Where the thin sun has less to squander
They hold strange course – remembering
And remembering where in the mind's map lie
The road and the mountain,
Islands of home
Pointing a finger at the near north's heart.

BERNARD SPENCER

Base Town

Winter's white guard continual on the hills;
The wind savaging from the stony valleys
And the unseen front. And always the soldiers going,
Soldiers and lorries beating the streets of cobble,
Like blood to where a wound is flowing.

War took friends, lights and names away. Clapped down
Shutters on windows' welcome. Brought those letters
Which wished to say so much they dared not say.
The proud and feminine ships in the harbour roads
Turned to a North-East grey.

Curious the intimacy we felt with Them;
We moved our meals to fit Their raids; we read
Their very hand across each bomb-slashed wall.
Their charred plane fallen in the cratered square
Held twisted in it all

Their work, Their hate, Their failure. Prisoners
Bearded and filthy, had bones, eyes and hair
Like other men in need. But dead like snow,
Cold like those racing winds or sirens' grief,
Was the hate which struck no blow:

The fear of speaking was a kind of tic
Pulling at the eyes. If stranger drank with stranger
It seemed thief drank with thief. Was it only every
Night, the fall of the early and lampless dark?
I remember it so often. And the lie,
The twist of reason,
The clever rumour planted in the nerves,
The dossier infecting like a coccus;
All these became for us the town, the season.

These, and the knowledge that to die,
Some stony miles north of our wintering
Was a more ordinary thing.

KEITH DOUGLAS

Christodoulos

Christodoulos moves, and shakes
his seven chins. He is that freak
a successful alchemist, and makes
God knows how much a week.

Out of Christodoulos' attic,
full of smoke and smells, emerge
soldiers like ants; with ants' erratic
gestures seek the pavement's verge;

weak as wounded, leaning in a knot
shout in the streets for an enemy –
the dross of Christodoulos' pot
or wastage from his alchemy.

They flow elsewhere; by swarthy portals
entering the crucibles of others
and the lesser sages' mortars:
but Christodoulos is the father

of all, he's the original wise one
from whose experiments they told
how War can be the famous stone
for turning rubbish into gold.

Egypt, September 1942

CHARLES CAUSLEY

Recruiting Drive

Under the willow the willow
　　I heard the butcher-bird sing,
Come out you fine young fellow
　　From under your mother's wing.
I'll show you the magic garden
　　That hangs in the beamy air,
The way of the lynx and the angry Sphinx
　　And the fun of the freezing fair.

Lie down lie down with my daughter
　　Beneath the Arabian tree,
Gaze on your face in the water
　　Forget the scribbling sea.
Your pillow the nine bright shiners
　　Your bed in the spilling sand,
But the terrible toy of my lily-white-boy
　　Is the gun in his innocent hand.

You must take off your clothes for the doctor
　　And stand as straight as a pin,
His hand of stone on your white breast-bone
　　Where the bullets all go in.
They'll dress you in lawn and linen
　　And fill you with Plymouth gin,
O the devil may wear a rose in his hair
　　I'll wear my fine doe-skin.

My mother weeps as I leave her
　　But I tell her it won't be long,
The murderers wail in Wandsworth Gaol
　　But I shoot a more popular song.
Down in the enemy country
　　Under the enemy tree
There lies a lad whose heart has gone bad
　　Waiting for me, for me.

He says I have no culture
 And that when I've stormed the pass
I shall fall on the farm with a smoking arm
 And ravish his bonny lass.
Under the willow the willow
 Death spreads her dripping wings
And caught in the snare of the bleeding air
 The butcher-bird sings, sings, sings.

HOWARD NEMEROV

Grand Central, With Soldiers, In Early Morning

These secretly are going to some place,
Packing their belted, serviceable hearts.
It is the earnest wish of this command
That they may go in stealth and leave no trace,
In early morning before business starts.

ROBERT GARIOCH

Hysteria

Left! Richt! Left turn! Richt turn! Richt about turn!
I birl, thinking nae mair nor I maun.
For this is meant to reive me of my wits;
they need me as a nummer, no a man.

And yet, it's no owre difficult to lauch
and niver to be nabb'd. They cannae hear
yir snockrin for the bashing of the buitts.
Ha-ha! They'll niver drive me gyte, nae fear!

Buckl't, ha-ha! frae brechan til the haims
to fettle me, ha-ha! frae hernia,
wi mask and killing-gear, ha-ha! I birl,
Left turn! Richt turn! Richt about turn! Ah! Ah!

EVGENY VINOKUROV

Missing the Troop Train

There's something desperate about trains . . .
I stood alone on the icy platform,
Lost in the Bashkir steppes.
What can be more fantastic, more desolate
Than the light of an electric lamp
Rocking in a small station at night?
Trains swept past from time to time.
Their roar engulfed me,
I was submerged in coal dust,
And each time, I grabbed hold of my cap –
It looked as though I was greeting someone.
The bare, stunted tree by the side of the platform
Reached out after them . . .
I waited for one train at least
To stop, for God's sake!
In the distance was the dark forest mass.
I lifted my head –
Over me, a vast
Host of stars:
Regiments,
        divisions,
                armies of stars,
All bound for somewhere.
An hour earlier, I'd got out of the train
To fetch some boiling water . . .
I could be court-martialled for this.
I stood there,
The snow melted round my boots,
And the water in the aluminium kettle I was holding
Had already iced over.
Above the forest mass, I saw
A little star,
Fallen a long way behind the others.
I looked at it
And it looked at me.

translated by A. Rudolf and D. Weissbort

RANDALL JARRELL

Mail Call

The letters always just evade the hand.
One skates like a stone into a beam, falls like a bird.
Surely the past from which the letters rise
Is waiting in the future, past the graves?
The soldiers are all haunted by their lives.

Their claims upon their kind are paid in paper
That establishes a presence, like a smell.
In letters and dreams they see the world.
They are waiting: and the years contract
To an empty hand, to one unuttered sound –

The soldier simply wishes for his name.

F. T. PRINCE

Soldiers Bathing

The sea at evening moves across the sand.
Under a reddening sky I watch the freedom of a band
Of soldiers who belong to me. Stripped bare
For bathing in the sea, they shout and run in the warm air;
Their flesh worn by the trade of war, revives
And my mind towards the meaning of it strives.

All's pathos now. The body that was gross,
Rank, ravenous, disgusting in the act or in repose,
All fever, filth and sweat, its bestial strength
And bestial decay, by pain and labour grows at length
Fragile and luminous. 'Poor bare forked animal',
Conscious of his desires and needs and flesh that rise and fall,
Stands in the soft air, tasting after toil
The sweetness of his nakedness: letting the sea-waves coil

Their frothy tongues about his feet, forgets
His hatred of the war, its terrible pressure that begets
A machinery of death and slavery,
Each being a slave and making slaves of others: finds that he
Remembers his old freedom in a game
Mocking himself, and comically mimics fear and shame.

He plays with death and animality;
And reading in the shadow of his pallid flesh, I see
The idea of Michelangelo's cartoon
Of soldiers bathing, breaking off before they were half done
At some sortie of the enemy, an episode
Of the Pisan wars with Florence. I remember how he showed
Their muscular limbs that clamber from the water,
And heads that turn across the shoulder, eager for the slaughter,
Forgetful of their bodies that are bare,
And hot to buckle on and use the weapons lying there.
– And I think too of the theme another found
When, shadowing men's bodies on a sinister red ground,
Another Florentine, Pollaiuolo,
Painted a naked battle: warriors, straddled, hacked the foe,
Dug their bare toes into the ground and slew
The brother-naked man who lay between their feet and drew
His lips back from his teeth in a grimace.

They were Italians who knew war's sorrow and disgrace
And showed the thing suspended, stripped: a theme
Born out of the experience of war's horrible extreme
Beneath a sky where even the air flows
With *lacrimae Christi*. For that rage, that bitterness, those blows,
That hatred of the slain, what could they be
But indirectly or directly a commentary
On the Crucifixion? And the picture burns
With indignation and pity and despair by turns,
Because it is the obverse of the scene
Where Christ hangs murdered, stripped, upon the Cross. I mean,
That is the explanation of its rage.

And we too have our bitterness and pity that engage
Blood, spirit, in this war. But night begins,

[33]

Night of the mind: who nowadays is conscious of our sins?
Though every human deed concerns our blood,
And even we must know, what nobody has understood,
That some great love is over all we do,
And that is what has driven us to this fury, for so few
Can suffer all the terror of that love:
The terror of that love has set us spinning in this groove
Greased with our blood.

                These dry themselves and dress,
Combing their hair, forget the fear and shame of nakedness.
Because to love is frightening we prefer
The freedom of our crimes. Yet, as I drink the dusky air,
I feel a strange delight that fills me full,
Strange gratitude, as if evil itself were beautiful,
And kiss the wound in thought, while in the west
I watch a streak of red that might have issued from
      Christ's breast.

HOWARD NEMEROV

Song

Provide your friend with almanacs
And cast him up a horoscope
Suggest the future that he lacks
Would have supplied his hopes

Give him beer and several wives
Good books and blankets for the trip
With stuff enough for fifty lives
Flatter his mortalship

Lay his weapons by his side
His address book and telephone
Try to convince him of the pride
Felt by the folks back home

And write him letters now and then
Be sure to put them in the post
Sound as cheerful as you can
Care of the holy ghost

Like anyone gone overseas
He'll take kindly to your talk
There in the camp beneath the trees
Where the sentry worms walk

ALAN ROSS

Mess Deck

The bulkhead sweating, and under naked bulbs
Men writing letters, playing Ludo. The light
Cuts their arms off at the wrist, only the dice
Lives. Hammocks swing, nuzzling-in tight
Like foals into flanks of mares. Bare shoulders
Glisten with oil, tattoo-marks rippling their scales on
Mermaids of girls' thighs as dice are shaken, cards played.
We reach for sleep like a gas, randy for oblivion.
But, laid out on lockers, some get waylaid;
And lie stiff, running off films in the mind's dark-room.
The air soupy, yet still cold; a beam sea rattles
Cups smelling of stale tea, knocks over a broom.
The light is watery, like the light of the sea-bed;
Marooned in it, stealthy as fishes, we may even be dead.

ALUN LEWIS

The Sentry

I have begun to die.
For now at last I know
That there is no escape
From Night. Not any dream

Nor breathless images of sleep
Touch my bat's-eyes. I hang
Leathery-arid from the hidden roof
Of Night, and sleeplessly
I watch within Sleep's province.
I have left
The lovely bodies of the boy and girl
Deep in each other's placid arms;
And I have left
The beautiful lanes of sleep
That barefoot lovers follow to this last
Cold shore of thought I guard.
I have begun to die
And the guns' implacable silence
Is my black interim, my youth and age,
In the flower of fury, the folded poppy,
Night.

JOHANNES BOBROWSKI

Lake Ilmen 1941

Wilderness. Against the wind.
Numb. The river sunk
into the sand.
Charred branches:
the village before the clearing. Then
we saw the lake –

– Days of the lake. Of light.
A track in the grass,
the white tower stands
like a gravestone
deserted by the dead.
The broken roof
in the caw of crows.
– Nights of the lake. The forest
falls into the marshes.

The old wolf,
fat from the burnt-out site,
startled by a phantom.
– Years of the lake. The armoured
flood. The climbing darkness
of the waters. One day
it will strike
the storming birds from the sky.

Did you see the sail? Fire
stood in the distance. The
wolf crossed the clearing.
Listens for the bells of winter.
Howls for the enormous
cloud of snow.

translated by Ruth and Matthew Mead

KAORU MARUYAMA

Gun Emplacement

Bits of shrapnel trying to huddle together:
A crack trying to burst its bonds:
A gun-barrel trying to rise
And sit on its carriage again.
Everything, dreaming of its passing original form
Was buried in sand with each blast.
Out of sight, the sea,
And the flickering gleam of migrating birds.

translated by Geoffrey Bownas and Anthony Thwaite

BERTRAM WARR

The Heart to Carry On

Every morning from this home
I go to the aerodrome

And at evening I return
Save when work is to be done.
Then we share the separate night
Half a continent apart.

Many endure worse than we:
Division means by years and seas.
Home and lover are contained,
Even cursed within their breast.

Leaving you now, with this kiss
May your sleep tonight be blest,
Shielded from the heart's alarms
Until morning I return.
Pray tomorrow I may be
Close, my love, within these arms,
And not lie dead in Germany.

ROBERT GARIOCH

Property

A man should have no thought for property,
he said, and drank down his pint.
Mirage is found in the Desert and elsewhere.
Later, in Libya (sand & scrub,
the sun two weeks to midsummer)
he carried all his property over the sand:
socks, knife and spoon, a dixie,
toilet kit, the Works of Shakespeare,
blanket, groundsheet, greatcoat,
and a water-bottle holding no more water.
He walked with other scorched men
in the dryness of this littoral waste land,
a raised beach without even sea water
with a much damned escarpment
unchanged throughout a day's truck-bumping
or a lifetime of walking without water,
confirming our worst fears of eternity.

[38]

Two men only went on whistling,
skidding on a beat-frequency.
Tenderness to music's dissonances,
and much experience of distress in art
was distressed, this time, in life.
A hot dry wind rose, moving the sand,
the sand-shifting Khamsin, rustling over
the land, whistling through hardy sandy
scrub, where sand-snails' brittle
shells on the sand, things in themselves,
roll for ever. Suffusing the sand in the
air, the sun burned in darkness.
No man now whistled, only the sandy wind.
The greatcoat first, then blanket discarded
and the other property lay absurd on the Desert,
but he kept his water-bottle.
In February, in a cold wet climate,
he has permanent damp in his bones
for lack of that groundsheet.
He has a different notion of the values of things.

SORLEY MACLEAN

Going Westwards

I go westwards in the Desert
with my shame on my shoulders
that I was made a laughing-stock
since I was as my people were.

Love and the greater error,
deceiving honour spoiled me,
with a film of weakness on my vision,
squinting at mankind's extremity.

Far from me the Island
when the moon rises on Quattara,
far from me the Pine Headland
when the morning ruddiness is on the Desert.

Camus Alba is far from me
and so is the bondage of Europe,
far from me in the North-West
the most beautiful grey-blue eyes.

Far from me the Island
and every loved image in Scotland,
there is a foreign sand in History
spoiling the machines of the mind.

Far from me Belsen and Dachau,
Rotterdam, the Clyde and Prague,
and Dimitrov before a court
hitting fear with the thump of his laugh.

Guernica itself is very far
from the innocent corpses of the Nazis,
who are lying in the gravel
and in the khaki sand of the Desert.

There is no rancour in my heart
against the hardy soldiers of the Enemy,
but the kinship that there is among
men in prison on a tidal rock

waiting for the sea flowing
and making cold the warm stone;
and the coldness of life (is)
in the hot sun of the Desert.

But this is the struggle not to be avoided,
the sore extreme of human-kind,
and though I do not hate Rommel's army
the brain's eye is not squinting.

And be what was as it was,
I am of the big men of Braes,
of the heroic Raasay MacLeods,
of the sharp-sword Mathesons of Lochalsh;
and the men of my name – who were braver
when their ruinous pride was kindled?

ALEXANDER TVARDOVSKY

from *Vassili Tyorkin: A Book About a Soldier*

DEATH AND THE SOLDIER

As the battle din receded
Over the hills and far away,
Tyorkin, lonely and unheeded,
In the snow abandoned lay.

Blood and snow to ice had hardened
Underneath him. Stealthily,
Death stooped over him and whispered:
'Soldier, come along with me.

'I am now your own dear true-love,
And we haven't far to go.
I shall make the blinding blizzard
Hide your trail with sifting snow.'

Tyorkin shuddered as he froze there
On his ice-encrusted bed.
'I don't need you here, *Kosaya*,*
I am still alive, not dead.'

Laughing, Death stooped lower, saying:
'Here, young fellow, that will do.
Though you live, your hours are numbered.
I know better far than you.

'As I passed, my deathly shadow
Touched your cheeks so young and fair,
And you haven't even noticed
How the snow is settling there.

'Do not fear my shades of darkness,
Truly, night's no worse than day....'
'What d'you mean? Just what exactly
Are you after, anyway?'

Here Death almost seemed to falter,
And she even half withdrew,
'I ask little, almost nothing. . . .
This is what I want of you:

'Just a token of agreement
That you're weary of this world,
That you pray for Death to free you. . . .'

'Sign my name, then, in a word?'
Death fell thoughtful:
'You could say that —
Sign for everlasting peace.'
'Go! I sell my life more dearly.'
'Don't you bargain, lovey, please!

'What's the use? Your strength is failing.'
Death drew closer, bent down low.
'What's the use? Your lips are freezing,
Cold your teeth. . . .'
'The answer's: No.'

translated by Alex Miller

*Death the Squint-Eyed. But female in Russian. *Trans*.

JOHN QUINN

Men Laughing

I had heard laughter when I was very young.
Long ages back I knew laughter,
And I laughed
(As men did)
At bedroom stories told in jostling bars,
Bellowed and shook at some Lothario's fall,
And went away feeling a mighty fellow.
Tittered politely at women's pretty tales,

Faintly indecent. And chuckled knowingly
At whispered scandals.
Laughed viciously,
Slung petty muck at many a pillory . . .
Far, far days
When laughter ruled,
And I laughed.
(Being very young – it was three years ago.)

That bleating, hollow laughter.

Now
I have heard soldiers laughing,
(You do not forget the sound of soldiers' laughter,
Deep, hard laughter, like anvils beaten in granite caves,)
Their challenge to blind, stupid fate,
Knowing her blindness,
Hating her blindness,
Mocking her blindness.

The laughter of soldiers.
Ghost echoes,
Sounding back from the grey desert,
Splitting across the red, bellowing air
Above Thermopylae,
Faint on the Syrian hills,
Crowing bitterly in lost Tobruk,
And crashing through torn, empty Darwin streets.

Laughing men on leave,
Filling old, arched streets with laughter,
Waking dim shades and stirring ancient temples
To thoughts that the Crusades had come again.
Kind laughter at children tumbling in the dust,
Laughter at the lovely, living things.

And in the smoking, blasted fields,
Tired laughter,
As at some joke enjoyed for overlong . . .

That jester, Life, that torment, merry rogue –
Such silent laughter at his latest prank,
Sprawled gutted, grinning at the sky.

HAMISH HENDERSON

Second Elegy: Halfaya

(FOR LUIGI CASTIGLIANO)

At dawn, under the concise razor-edge
of the escarpment, the laager sleeps. No petrol fires yet
blow flame for brew-up. Up on the pass a sentry
inhales his Nazionale. Horse-shoe curve of the bay
grows visible beneath him. He smokes and yawns.
Ooo-augh,
            and the limitless
shabby lion-pelt of the desert completes and rounds
his limitless ennui.

At dawn, in the gathering impetus of day, the laager sleeps.
Some restless princes dream: first light denies them
the luxury of nothing. But others their mates more lucky
drown in the lightless grottoes. (Companionable death has
    lent
them his ease for a moment.)
                The dreamers remember
a departure like a migration. They recall a landscape
associated with warmth and veils and pantomime
but never focused exactly. The flopping curtain
reveals scene-shifters running with freshly painted
incongruous sets. Here childhood's prairie garden
looms like a pampas, where grown-ups stalk (gross outlaws)
on legs of tree trunk: recedes: and the strepitant jungle
dwindles to scruff of shrubs on a docile common,
all but real for a moment, then gone.

The sleepers turn
gone but still no nothing laves them.
O misery, desire, desire, tautening cords of the bedrack!
Eros, in the teeth of Yahveh and his tight-lipped sect
confound the deniers of their youth! Let war lie wounded!
Eros, grant forgiveness and release
and return – against which they erect it,
the cairn of patience. *No dear, won't be long now*
keep fingers crossed, chin up, keep smiling darling
be seeing you soon.

On the horizon fires fluff now,
further than they seem.

Sollum and Halfaya
a while yet before we leave you in quiet
and our needle swings north.

The sleepers toss
and turn before waking: they feel through their blankets
the cold of the malevolent bomb-thumped desert,
impartial
hostile to both.

The laager is one.
Friends and enemies, haters and lovers
both sleep and dream.

RAYMOND SOUSTER

Army Reception Centre

That year they scraped the barrel
for the last awkward time
with us at the very bottom.

Farm kids in overalls
and laced-up boots,
a few city boys
with all the answers.

I remember reading Hemingway
in the smoky barracks,
waiting the call
for the gaze up the rectum,
the intelligence test,
the over-friendly examiner.

And every evening
walked over the bridge
across their wide river
to where the bad girls
were supposed to be.

While the newly-arrived
veterans of the far-off war
sat around in the corridors
with arms or legs missing
waiting for discharge:

(waiting being just
another name for the army).

Fredericton, 1944

HOWARD NEMEROV

A Fable of the War

The full moon is partly hidden by cloud,
The snow that fell when we came off the boat
Has stopped by now, and it is turning colder.
I pace the platform under the blue lights,
Under a frame of glass and emptiness
In a station whose name I do not know.

Suddenly, passing the known and unknown
Bowed faces of my company, the sad
And potent outfit of the armed, I see
That we are dead. By stormless Acheron
We stand easy, and the occasional moon
Strikes terribly from steel and bone alike.

Our flesh, I see, was too corruptible
For the huge work of death. Only the blind
Crater of the eye can suffer well
The midnight cold of stations in no place,
And hold the tears of pity frozen that
They will implacably reflect on war.

But I have read that God let Solomon
Stand upright, although dead, until the temple
Should be raised up, that demons forced to the work
Might not revolt before the thing was done.
And the king stood, until a little worm
Had eaten through the stick he leaned upon.

So, gentlemen – by greatcoat, cartridge belt
And helmet held together for the time –
In honorably enduring here we seek
The second death. Until the worm shall bite
To betray us, lean each man on his gun
That the great work not falter but go on.

III

---

*'Boswell by my bed,
Tolstoy on my table'*

WALLACE STEVENS

Martial Cadenza

I

Only this evening I saw again low in the sky
The evening star, at the beginning of winter, the star
That in spring will crown every western horizon,
Again . . . as if it came back, as if life came back,
Not in a later son, a different daughter, another place,
But as if evening found us young, still young,
Still walking in a present of our own.

II

It was like sudden time in a world without time,
This world, this place, the street in which I was,
Without time: as that which is not has no time,
Is not, or is of what there was, is full
Of the silence before the armies, armies without
Either trumpets or drums, the commanders mute, the arms
On the ground, fixed fast in profound defeat.

III

What had this star to do with the world it lit,
With the blank skies over England, over France
And above the German camps? It looked apart.
Yet it is this that shall maintain – Itself
Is time, apart from any past, apart
From any future, the ever-living and being,
The ever-breathing and moving, the constant fire,

IV

The present close, the present realized,
Not the symbol but that for which the symbol stands,
The vivid thing in the air that never changes,
Though the air change. Only this evening I saw it again,
At the beginning of winter, and I walked and talked
Again, and lived and was again, and breathed again
And moved again and flashed again, time flashed again.

[51]

EDMUND BLUNDEN

A Prospect of Swans

Walking the river way to change our note
From the hard season and from harder care,
    Marvelling we found the swans,
The swans on sullen swollen dykes afloat
Or moored on tussocks, a full company there,
White breasts and necks, advance and poise and stir
Filling the scene, while rays of steel and bronze
From the far dying sun touched the dead reeds.

So easy was the manner of each one,
So sure and wise the course of all their needs,
So free their unity, in that level sun
And floodland tipped with sedge and osiery,
It might have been where man was yet to be,
Some mere where none but swans were ever kings,
Where gulls might hunt, a wide flight in from sea,
And page-like small birds come: all innocent wings.

O picture of some first divine intent,
O young world which perhaps was modelled thus,
    Where even hard winter meant
No disproportion, hopeless hungers none,
And set no task which could not well be done.
Now this primeval pattern gleamed at us
Right near the town's black smoke-towers and the roar
Of trains bearing the sons of man to war.

The Failed Spirit

To those who are isolate
War comes, promising respite,
Making what seems to be up to the moment the most successful
        endeavour
Against the fort of the failed spirit that is alone for ever.
Spurious failed spirit, adamantine wasture,
Crop, spirit, crop thy stony pasture!

JUDITH WRIGHT

The Trains

Tunnelling through the night, the trains pass
in a splendour of power, with a sound like thunder
shaking the orchards, waking
the young from a dream, scattering like glass
the old men's sleep; laying
a black trail over the still bloom of the orchards.
The trains go north with guns.

Strange primitive piece of flesh, the heart laid quiet
hearing their cry pierce through its thin-walled cave
recalls the forgotten tiger
and leaps awake in its old panic riot;
and how shall mind be sober,
since blood's red thread still binds us fast in history?
Tiger, you walk through all our past and future,
troubling the children's sleep; laying
a reeking trail across our dream of orchards.

Racing on iron errands, the trains go by,
and over the white acres of our orchards
hurl their wild summoning cry, their animal cry ...
the trains go north with guns.

[53]

BERNARD SPENCER

Salonika June 1940

My end of Europe is at war. For this
My lamp-launched giant shadow seems to fall
Like a bad thought upon this ground at peace,
Being the shadow of the shadow of a war.
What difference if I wish good luck to these foreigners, my hosts?
Talking with my friends stand ghosts.

Specially the lives that here in the crook of this bay
At the paws of its lionish hills are lived as I know;
The dancing, the bathing, the order of the market, and as day
Cools into night, boys playing in the square;
Island boats and lemon-peel tang and the timeless café crowd,
And the outcry of dice on wood:

I would shut the whole if I could out of harm's way
As one shuts a holiday photo away in a desk,
Or shuts one's eyes. But not by this brilliant bay,
Nor in Hampstead now where leaves are green,
Any more exists a word or a lock which gunfire may not break,
Or a love whose range it may not take.

VLADIMÍR HOLAN

Human Voice

Stone and star do not force their music on us,
flowers are silent, things hold something back,
because of us, animals deny
their own harmony of innocence and stealth,
the wind has always its chastity of simple gesture
and what song is only the mute birds know,
to whom you tossed an unthreshed sheaf on Christmas Eve.

To be is enough for them and that is beyond words. But we,
we are afraid not only in the dark,

even in the abundant light
we do not see our neighbour
and desperate for exorcism
cry out in terror: 'Are you there? Speak!'

translated by Ian and Jarmila Miller

BORIS PASTERNAK

False Alarm

Cattle trough and bucket,
Confusion since dawn,
Rain squalls at sunset,
Damp evening coming on,

Tears choked down by dark sighs
In the dark hours before day,
A locomotive calling
From sixteen versts away

And early twilight
In backyard and garden,
And all those breakages . . .
September's here again!

By day the breadth of autumn
Is scissored by the shriek
Of heartstruck anguish
From the churchyard by the creek.

And when the widow's sobbing
Is carried along the bank,
My heart goes out to her
And I see death point-blank.

I see from the hall window.
Today as every year,
My long delayed last day
At last arriving here.

And clearing a way
Downhill through horrible
Decaying yellow leaves,
Winter stares at my skull.

1941
translated by Jon Stallworthy and Peter France

JUDITH WRIGHT

The Company of Lovers

We meet and part now over all the world.
We, the lost company,
take hands together in the night, forget
the night in our brief happiness, silently.
We who sought many things, throw all away
for this one thing, one only,
remembering that in the narrow grave
we shall be lonely.

Death marshals up his armies round us now.
Their footsteps crowd too near.
Lock your warm hand above the chilling heart
and for a time I live without my fear.
Grope in the night to find me and embrace,
for the dark preludes of the drums begin,
and round us, round the company of lovers,
Death draws his cordons in.

GYULA ILLYÉS

It is Five Years Now

It is five years now that you've been dead,
but from the grave you find your way—
nothing has changed – to the old café
where I waited for you, where last you waited
in the smoke-thatched gloom, in a corner where
you shivered as in some field lean-to;
the rain came down: we fought, we two;
and you were mad, but I didn't know then.

You're less than mad now; nothing has remained:
on the floor where time that danced so bright
has flown away, I sit mute, alone.

Absurd it is since you have gone:
the whole world seems to have gone mad—
and you, being mad, have won the fight.

1942
translated by William Jay Smith

JAROSLAV SEIFERT

Robed in Light

As I was walking in the fading light —
Prague seemed more beautiful than Rome to me —
I was afraid that from this dream I might
never awake, that I might never see
the stars that, when the daylight comes again,
beneath their folded wings the gargoyles hide —
the gargoyles standing, as on guard, beside
the cornice of St Vitus' ancient fane.

[57]

One morning in the early hours, too late
to go to bed – the dawn was drawing near —
I stood before the still unopened gate
of the great church, but would not knock for fear,
as a poor pilgrim, on a winter morn,
finding it shut, will stand beside a door;
I wished to see the gargoyles just before
they greet the stars returning home at dawn.

Instead I saw a tomb and went to view
the statue on it – all alone was I;
Like a wrecked ship appeared the dead man's shoe;
its toe was pointing upwards to the sky.
And as I looked a flickering candle flung
strange shadows on the tomb from head to heel;
it was as though I heard the spinning-wheel
and peasants' songs amid the vineyards sung.

The grapes are in the royal garment's weave,
in grey, as early-morning human breath,
four ladies sleeping in the Gothic nave
are carrying the dead man on their breasts.
Remember me to Karlštejn's woods, their pines
descending gently to the sunlit plains.
Remember me to Karlštejn's walls again
and to the hillsides clad in verdant vines!

From his tomb he raised above the pillars
(sprouting, so it seemed, out of his palms)
a blanched human skull; behold, a lover's
hands created for caress and charms
touched it and the touch lent it endurance
through a nation's song whose lips had cracked,
gave it strength, it was a secret pact
that was left of its inheritance.

Why, its lips from thirst were bound to numb —
ceaselessly it slept upon its sword —
through the ages rang the ancient hymn,
ardent song of safety and accord.

[58]

And the Saint, obscured now by the shapes
of wings of angels and the shield of prayer,
broke white bread among his country's poor
and with his own feet trod the firm white grapes.

In confusion I regard this majesty,
press into the beggars' shade nearby,
I'm not here to weep among the amethysts,
I have long forgotten how to cry.
The lace edge of the altarcloth was torn,
the music stand had spilled a few sheets:
through the long nave rang steps of heavy boots,
clicking darkly on the floor's mosaic.

translated by Ewald Osers

E. J. SCOVELL

Days Drawing In

The days fail: night broods over afternoon:
And at my child's first drink beyond the night
Her skin is silver in the early light.
Sweet the grey morning and the raiders gone.

GEORGE WOODCOCK

Pacifists

The icy, empty dawn cracks in the fields
Under our labouring feet. We cross the fallow
With billhooks on our shoulders sloped like guns,
Drawing dark lines in rime white as we go.

Standing in filthy ditches in leaking boots,
We fell the towering hedges like Jericho walls
Under the blast of day. Around our feet
The water seeps and numbs through invisible holes.

Strange we have come, from library and office.
Hands that had never toiled, myopic eyes
And sloping backs revolt in an alien time.
Under a dead sky we expiate our oddness.

Having left friends and substitutes for love
In the leaning fragments of a distant city
We tread the furrows of infertile fields
And rediscover our pasts in a wet country.

Under our ineffectual misery, our boredom
And the empty sequence of unprivate days,
The lost squalors of the city become our end.
The cause that brought us dwindles. We hate blank skies,

Biting wind and the black bones of trees,
The promise of spring as a green omen of toil.
We rest our billhooks and talk of starlit town
As the weak sun breaks on the land without a hill.

1975

HD

From *The Walls do not Fall*

An incident here and there,
and rails gone (for guns)
from your (and my) old town square:

mist and mist-grey, no colour,
still the Luxor bee, chick and hare
pursue unalterable purpose

in green, rose-red, lapis;
they continue to prophesy
from the stone papyrus:

there, as here, ruin opens
the tomb, the temple; enter,
there as here, there are no doors:

the shrine lies open to the sky,
the rain falls, here, there
sand drifts; eternity endures:

ruin everywhere, yet as the fallen roof
leaves the sealed room
open to the air,

so, through our desolation,
thoughts stir, inspiration stalks us
through gloom:

unaware, Spirit announces the Presence;
shivering overtakes us,
as of old, Samuel:

trembling at a known street-corner,
we know not nor are known;
the Pythian pronounces – we pass on

to another cellar, to another sliced wall
where poor utensils show
like rare objects in a museum;

Pompeii has nothing to teach us,
we know crack of volcanic fissure,
slow flow of terrible lava,

pressure on heart, lungs, the brain
about to burst its brittle case
(what the skull can endure!):

over us, Apocryphal fire,
under us, the earth sway, dip of a floor,
slope of a pavement

where men roll, drunk
with a new bewilderment,
sorcery, bedevilment:

the bone-frame was made for
no such shock knit within terror,
yet the skeleton stood up to it:

the flesh? it was melted away,
the heart burnt out, dead ember,
tendons, muscles shattered, outer husk
    dismembered

yet the frame held:
we passed the flame: we wonder
what saved us? what for?

1942

ANNA AKHMATOVA

from *In 1940*

TO THE LONDONERS

Time is writing Shakespeare's twenty-fourth drama,
with a clear, dispassionate hand,
and for us, the partakers of this menacing feast,
it is better to read *Hamlet, Julius Caesar* or *King Lear*
by the molten lead river.
Better for us today to accompany the little dove Juliet
to the grave with torches and singing,
better to look through the window at Macbeth
and tremble with the hired murderer,
but not this, not this, not this,
this even we aren't capable of reading.

translated by Richard McKane

EDITH SITWELL

Still Falls the Rain

(THE RAIDS, 1940. NIGHT AND DAWN)

STILL falls the Rain —
Dark as the world of man, black as our loss —
Blind as the nineteen hundred and forty nails
Upon the Cross.

Still falls the Rain
With a sound like the pulse of the heart that is changed to
   the hammer-beat
In the Potter's Field, and the sound of the impious feet

On the Tomb:
               Still falls the Rain
In the Field of Blood where the small hopes breed and
   the human brain
Nurtures its greed, that worm with the brow of Cain.

Still falls the Rain
At the feet of the Starved Man hung upon the Cross.
Christ that each day, each night, nails there, have mercy
   on us —
On Dives and on Lazarus:
Under the Rain the sore and the gold are as one.

Still falls the Rain —
Still falls the Blood from the Starved Man's wounded Side:
He bears in His Heart all wounds, — those of the light
   that died,
The last faint spark
In the self-murdered heart, the wounds of the sad
   uncomprehending dark,
The wounds of the baited bear, —
The blind and weeping bear whom the keepers beat
On his helpless flesh . . . the tears of the hunted hare.

Still falls the Rain —
Then — O Ile leape up to my God: who pulles me
  doune —
See, see where Christ's blood streames in the firmament:
It flows from the Brow we nailed upon the tree
Deep to the dying, to the thirsting heart
That holds the fires of the world, — dark-smirched with
  pain
At Caesar's laurel crown.

Then sounds the voice of One who like the heart of man
Was once a child who among beasts has lain —
'Still do I love, still shed my innocent light, my Blood,
  for thee.'

ALLEN TATE

Ode to Our Young Pro-consuls of the Air

TO ST-JOHN PERSE

Once more the country calls
From sleep, as from his doom,
  Each citizen to take
  His modest stake
Where the sky falls
With a Pacific boom.

Warm winds in even climes
Push southward angry bees
  As we, with tank and plane,
  Wrest land and main
From yellow mimes,
The puny Japanese.

Boys hide in lunging cubes
Crouching to explode,
  Beyond Atlantic skies,
  With cheerful cries
Their barking tubes
Upon the German toad.

[64]

Marvelling day by day
Upon the human kind
   What might I have done
   (A poet alone)
To balk or slay
These enemies of mind?

I sought by night to foal
Chimeras into men –
   Decadence of power
   That, at late hour,
Untimed the soul
To live the past again:

Toy sword, three-cornered hat
At York and Lexington –
   While *Bon-Homme* whipped at sea
   This enemy
Whose roar went flat
After George made him run;

Toy rifle, leather hat
Above the boyish beard –
   And in that Blue renown
   The Gray went down,
Down like a rat,
And even the rats cheered.

In a much later age
(Europe had been in flames)
   Proud Wilson yielded ground
   To franc and pound,
Made pilgrimage
In the wake of Henry James.

Where Lou Quatorze held *fête*
For sixty thousand men,
   France took the German sword
   But later, bored,
Opened the gate
To Hitler – at Compiégne.

In this bad time no part
The poet took, nor chance:
    He studied Swift and Donne,
    Ignored the Hun,
While with faint heart
Proust caused the fall of France.

Sad day at Oahu
When the Jap beetle hit!
    Our Proustian retort
    Was Kimmel and Short,
Old women in blue,
And then the beetle bit.

It was defeat, or near it!
Yet all that feeble time
    Brave Brooks and lithe MacLeish
    Had sworn to thresh
Our flagging spirit
With literature made Prime!

Cow Creek and bright Bear Wallow,
Nursing the blague that dulls
    Spirits grown Eliotic,
    Now patriotic
Are: we follow
The Irresponsibles!

Young men, Americans!
You go to win the world
    With zeal pro-consular
    For our whole star –
You partisans
Of liberty unfurled!

O animal excellence,
Take pterodactyl flight
    Fire-winged into the air
    And find your lair
With cunning sense
On some Arabian bight

Or sleep your dreamless sleep
(Reptilian bomber!) by
   The Mediterranean
   And like a man
Swear you to keep
Faith with imperial eye:

Take off, O gentle youth,
And coasting India
   Scale crusty Everest
   Whose mythic crest
Resists your truth;
And spying far away

Upon the Tibetan plain
A limping caravan,
   Dive, and exterminate
   The Lama, late
Survival of old pain.
Go kill the dying swan.

1943

STEPHEN SPENDER

Air Raid Across The Bay At Plymouth

I

Above the whispering sea
And waiting rocks of black coast,
Across the bay, the searchlight beams
Swing and swing back across the sky.

Their ends fuse in a cone of light
Held for a bright instant up
Until they break away again
Smashing that image like a cup.

[67]

II

Delicate aluminium girders
Project phantom aerial masts
Swaying crane and derrick
Above the sea's just lifting deck.

III

Triangles, parallels, parallelograms,
Experiment with hypotheses
On the blackboard sky,
Seeking that X
Where the enemy is met.
Two beams cross
To chalk his cross.

IV

A sound, sounding ragged, unseen
Is chased by two swords of light.
A thud. An instant when the whole night gleams.
Gold sequins shake out of a black-silk screen.

V

Jacob ladders slant
Up to the god of war
Who, from his heaven-high car,
Unloads upon a star
A destroying star.

Round the coast, the waves
Chuckle between rocks.
In the fields the corn
Sways, with metallic clicks.
Man hammers nails in Man,
High on his crucifix.

ELIZABETH BISHOP

View of the Capitol from the Library of Congress

Moving from left to left, the light
is heavy on the Dome, and coarse.
One small lunette turns it aside
and blankly stares off to the side
like a big white old wall-eyed horse.

On the east steps the Air Force Band
in uniforms of Air Force blue
is playing hard and loud, but – queer –
the music doesn't quite come through.

It comes in snatches, dim then keen,
then mute, and yet there is no breeze.
The giant trees stand in between.
I think the trees must intervene,

catching the music in their leaves
like gold-dust, till each big leaf sags.
Unceasingly the little flags
feed their limp stripes into the air,
and the band's efforts vanish there.

Great shades, edge over,
give the music room.
The gathered brasses want to go
boom – boom.

DYLAN THOMAS

A Refusal to Mourn the Death, by Fire, of a Child in London

Never until the mankind making
Bird beast and flower
Fathering and all humbling darkness
Tells with silence the last light breaking
And the still hour
Is come of the sea tumbling in harness

And I must enter again the round
Zion of the water bead
And the synagogue of the ear of corn
Shall I let pray the shadow of a sound
Or sow my salt seed
In the least valley of sackcloth to mourn

The majesty and burning of the child's death.
I shall not murder
The mankind of her going with a grave truth
Nor blaspheme down the stations of the breath
With any further
Elegy of innocence and youth.

Deep with the first dead lies London's daughter,
Robed in the long friends,
The grains beyond age, the dark veins of her mother,
Secret by the unmourning water
Of the riding Thames.
After the first death, there is no other.

EDWIN MUIR

Reading in Wartime

Boswell by my bed,
Tolstoy on my table;
Though the world has bled

For four and a half years,
And wives' and mothers' tears
Collected would be able
To water a little field
Untouched by anger and blood,
A penitential yield
Somewhere in the world;
Though in each latitude
Armies like forests fall,
The iniquitous and the good
Head over heels hurled,
And confusion over all:
Boswell's turbulent friend
And his deafening verbal strife,
Ivan Ilych's death
Tell me more about life,
The meaning and the end
Of our familiar breath,
Both being personal,
Than all the carnage can,
Retrieve the shape of man,
Lost and anonymous,
Tell me wherever I look
That not one soul can die
Of this or any clan
Who is not one of us
And has a personal tie
Perhaps to someone now
Searching an ancient book,
Folk-tale or country song
In many and many a tongue,
To find the original face,
The individual soul,
The eye, the lip, the brow
For ever gone from their place,
And gather an image whole.

RACHEL KORN

Arthur Ziegelboim

When was it sealed, when was it decreed,
Your great, your wonderful deathless deed?
Did it come to you like a child in your dream?
Or did a dark messenger bring you the tale,
In your London exile?

Did the messenger come to your door, and knock,
A woman heavily shrouded in black—
'I come from the Warsaw Ghetto, where the earth is on fire!'
Her clothes in rags, a tattered shroud,
And her lips red with blood.

Then you knocked at doors, and found hearts that were closed.
You tried to rouse them, but they wouldn't be roused.
What people were those who refused to listen,
When children were gassed and flung on the mound?
And no one raised a hand!

You carried round stacks of papers to show.
'You may be right,' they said, 'but how can we know?
We want to believe you. But these are not facts.
And we are bound by conventions and acts.'

You brought out a list of the dead.
'How can you prove they are dead?' they said.
So to convince them, you added your name to the list.
You always gave proofs, like a realist.

One May night, when the orchards ripened in the land,
And Spring walked around with stars, hand in hand.
One window in a London street showed a light.
That was you, sitting down alone, to write.

You wrote your last letters, and your last Testament,
For the dawn to read, before the night was spent.
Then a shot rang out, a single shot
To wipe out the shame of which you wrote.
You died to make the world listen to the cry
From the Warsaw Ghetto, across the sky.

translated by Joseph Leftwich

WILLIAM MONTGOMERIE

The Edge of the War
(*1939–*)

On the esplanade
the deck-chair hirer
watches his summer
shovelled into sandbags
till at high tide
the beach is flooded to the Promenade

Our submarines like five alligators
pass
always at dusk
to the North Sea
where a German plane has sown surface mines

One mine circles the harbour slowly
missing the pier
again and again and again
until defused by a simple twist of the wrist

The whelk-seller leaves his bag and barrow
to pull a mine up the beach
and dies
'Stretchers! Stretchers here!'
they shout from the Castle

[73]

A policeman arrests one mine on the shore
and drags it halfway to the police-station
his tombstone a cottage gable-end
pocked with holes packed with red putty

Casks of brandy butter and ham
float on to the beach
from a mined ship

A grocer's van parks at dusk
by the Castle railings

Sergeant MacPherson pins on his notice-board
'Flotsam butter from the beach
must be left immediately
at the police-station'

For days the streets are sweet
with the smell of shortbread

Blue-mould butter
is dumped on the counter
or thrown at night
over the wall of the station
where greased door-handles will not turn

A German plane
following the wrong railway
dumps his bombs on an up-country farm

A plane from the North-Sea sunrise
machine-gunning our little fishing fleet
brushes a wing against a mast
and ditches

'Hilfe! Hilfe!'

'Take your time lads!'
shouts a skipper
to a drifter turning toward the sinking plane

'One of our planes
has sunk a German U-boat
off Montrose'

A war-rumour

The submarine
one of ours
dented
is in dry-dock
in Dundee

Bennet from Stratford-on-Avon
one of the crew
cycles to our house
with no lights
sings to us
of Boughton's Lordly Ones
from *The Immortal Hour*
talks of his wife in Stratford
and of the night they watched Birmingham burning

After late supper
he returns to the night
having left his ration of pipe-tobacco
on the piano

If his submarine sinks
he knows how to escape
and is found afloat
on the Pacific Ocean
drowned

On Tents Muir
across the Tay estuary
parachutes are falling
from war planes

We talk of the Second Front

One parachute does not open

Broughty Ferry

IV

*'Wounded no doubt and
pale from battle'*

RICHARD WILBUR

First Snow in Alsace

The snow came down last night like moths
Burned on the moon; it fell till dawn,
Covered the town with simple cloths.

Absolute snow lies rumpled on
What shellbursts scattered and deranged,
Entangled railings, crevassed lawn.

As if it did not know they'd changed,
Snow smoothly clasps the roofs of homes
Fear-gutted, trustless and estranged.

The ration stacks are milky domes;
Across the ammunition pile
The snow has climbed in sparkling combs.

You think: beyond the town a mile
Or two, this snowfall fills the eyes
Of soldiers dead a little while.

Persons and persons in disguise,
Walking the new air white and fine,
Trade glances quick with shared surprise.

At children's windows, heaped, benign,
As always, winter shines the most,
And frost makes marvellous designs.

The night-guard coming from his post,
Ten first-snows back in thought, walks slow
And warms him with a boyish boast:

He was the first to see the snow.

PETER HUCHEL

Roads

Choked sunset glow
Of crashing time.
Roads. Roads.
Intersections of flight.
Cart tracks across the ploughed field
That with the eyes
Of killed horses
Saw the sky in flames.

Nights with lungs full of smoke,
With the hard breath of the fleeing
When shots
Struck the dusk.
Out of a broken gate
Ash and wind came without a sound,
A fire
That sullenly chewed the darkness.

Corpses,
Flung over the rail tracks,
Their stifled cry
Like a stone on the palate.
A black
Humming cloth of flies
Closed their wounds.

translated by Michael Hamburger

DRUMMOND ALLISON

Frederick II in Sicily

From the now ghostly groves above Palermo
I see the smoke approaching, and I see
Another wave of race and anguish washing
On over Sicily.

Here in the heat, not in the sonorous northern
Cavern, my deadness has unholy home;
While the same indistinguishable strangers
Go to their graves or Rome.

Mahmud and Christ told lovely lies before them
– I learned it's only true that always men's
Guesses and wars are wrong, if Pope or Emperor,
English or Saracens.

SORLEY MACLEAN

Heroes

I did not see Lannes at Ratisbon
nor MacLennan at Auldearn
nor Gillies MacBain at Culloden,
but I saw an Englishman in Egypt.

A poor little chap with chubby cheeks
and knees grinding each other,
pimply unattractive face –
garment of the bravest spirit.

He was not a hit 'in the pub
in the time of the fists being closed,'
but a lion against the breast of battle,
in the morose wounding showers.

His hour came with the shells,
with the notched iron splinters.
in the smoke and flame,
in the shaking and terror of the battlefield.

Word came to him in the bullet shower
that he should be a hero briskly,
and he was that while he lasted
but it wasn't much time he got.

He kept his guns to the tanks,
bucking with tearing crashing screech,
until he himself got, about the stomach,
that biff that put him to the ground,
mouth down in sand and gravel,
without a chirp from his ugly high-pitched voice.

No cross or medal was put to his
chest or to his name or to his family;
there were not many of his troop alive,
and if there were their word would not be strong.
And at any rate, if a battle post stands
many are knocked down because of him,
not expecting fame, not wanting a medal
or any froth from the mouth of the field of slaughter.

I saw a great warrior of England,
a poor manikin on whom no eye would rest;
no Alasdair of Glen Garry;
and he took a little weeping to my eyes.

KEITH DOUGLAS

Cairo Jag

Shall I get drunk or cut myself a piece of cake,
a pasty Syrian with a few words of English
or the Turk who says she is a princess – she dances
apparently by levitation? Or Marcelle, Parisienne
always preoccupied with her dull dead lover:
she has all the photographs and his letters
tied in a bundle and stamped *Décéde* in mauve ink.
All this takes place in a stink of jasmine.

But there are the streets dedicated to sleep
stenches and the sour smells, the sour cries
do not disturb their application to slumber
all day, scattered on the pavement like rags

afflicted with fatalism and hashish. The women
offering their children brown-paper breasts
dry and twisted, elongated like the skull,
Holbein's signature. But this stained white town
is something in accordance with mundane conventions –
Marcelle drops her Gallic airs and tragedy
suddenly shrieks in Arabic about the fare
with the cabman, links herself so
with the somnambulists and legless beggars:
it is all one, all as you have heard.

But by a day's travelling you reach a new world
the vegetation is of iron
dead tanks, gun barrels split like celery
the metal brambles have no flowers or berries
and there are all sorts of manure, you can imagine
the dead themselves, their boots, clothes and possessions
clinging to the ground, a man with no head
has a packet of chocolate and a souvenir of Tripoli.

El Ballah, General hospital, February 1943

ROBERT GARIOCH

Letter from Italy

From large red bugs, a refugee,
I make my bed beneath the sky,
safe from the crawling enemy
though not secure from nimbler flea.
Late summer darkness comes, and now
I see again the homely Plough
and wonder: do you also see
the seven stars as well as I?
And it is good to find a tie
of seven stars from you to me.
Lying on deck, on friendly seas,
I used to watch, with no delight,

new unsuggestive stars that light
the tedious Antipodes.
Now in a hostile land I lie,
but share with you these ancient high
familiar named divinities.
Perimeters have bounded me,
sad rims of desert and of sea,
the famous one around Tobruk,
and now barbed wire, which way I look,
except above – the Pleiades.

NOBUO AYUKAWA

Saigon 1943

Not a soul on the quay.
No one had come to greet our ship.
The French town I'd dreamed of
floating on a colonial sea.
No trace here of the Orient.

Wrapped in white cloth
a corpse was carried unsteadily from the hatch –
a young army clerk
who'd killed himself with an open razor.

This was our Saigon.
France's anguish
was this city's anguish.
Could there be a connection
between the torment we as soldiers feel
and that of our fatherland?
Above the liners flying the Tricolore
was the serene blue sky
of a defeated country ripped by war.
With so many friends already dead,
so many others going off to die,
sick soldiers told the recent voiceless dead
how black the worms were
crawling beneath their living skin.

A light breeze was blowing.
With the same razor that had freed his soul
applied to our own thin throats,
we watched the dinghy carrying the stretcher
recede into the distance
parting the green water.

translated by Hajime Kajima

EDWIN MORGAN

from *The New Divan*

I dreaded stretcher-bearing,
my fingers would slip on the two sweat-soaked
    handles,
my muscles not used to the strain.
The easiest trip of all I don't forget,
in the desert, that dead officer
drained of blood, wasted away,
leg amputated at the thigh,
wrapped in a rough sheet, light as a child,
rolling from side to side of the canvas
with a faint terrible sound
as our feet stumbled through the sand.

NORMAN HAMPSON

Assault Convoy

How quietly they push the flat sea from them,
Shadows against the night, that grow to meet us
And fade back slowly to our zig-zag rhythm –
The silent pattern dim destroyers weave.
The first light greets them friendly; pasteboard ships

Erect in lineless mists of sky and sea.
A low sun lingers on the well-known outlines
That take new beauty from this sombre war-paint;
Familiar names trail childish memories
Of peace time ports and waving, gay departures.

Only at intervals the truth breaks on us
Like catspaws, ruffling these quiet waters.
Our future is unreal, a thing to read of
Later; a chapter in a history book.
We cannot see the beaches where the dead
Must fall before this waxing moon is full;
The tracer-vaulted sky, the gun's confusion,
Searchlights and shouted orders, sweaty fumbling
As landing craft are lowered; the holocaust
Grenade and bayonet will build upon these beaches.

We are dead, numbed, atrophied, sunk in the swamps of war.
Each of those thousands is a life entire.
No skilful smile can hide their sheer humanity.
Across the narrowing seas our enemies wait,
Each man the centre of his darkening world;
Bound, as we are, by humanity's traces of sorrow
To anxious women, alone in the menacing night,
Where the rhythm of Europe is lost in their private fear
And El Dorado cannot staunch their grief.

CHARLES CAUSLEY

Song of the Dying Gunner

Oh mother my mouth is full of stars
As cartridges in the tray
My blood is a twin-branched scarlet tree
And it runs all runs away.

[86]

Oh *Cooks to the Galley* is sounded off
And the lads are down in the mess
But I lie done by the forrard gun
With a bullet in my breast.

Don't send me a parcel at Christmas time
Of socks and nutty and wine
And don't depend on a long weekend
By the Great Western Railway line.

Farewell, Aggie Weston, the Barracks at Guz,
Hang my tiddley suit on the door
I'm sewn up neat in a canvas sheet
And I shan't be home no more.

RICHARD EBERHART

The Fury of Aerial Bombardment

You would think the fury of aerial bombardment
Would rouse God to relent; the infinite spaces
Are still silent. He looks on shock-pried faces.
History, even, does not know what is meant.

You would feel that after so many centuries
God would give man to repent; yet he can kill
As Cain could, but with multitudinous will,
No farther advanced than in his ancient furies.

Was man made stupid to see his own stupidity?
Is God by definition indifferent, beyond us all?
Is the eternal truth man's fighting soul
Wherein the Beast ravens in its own avidity?

Of Van Wettering I speak, and Averill,
Names on a list, whose faces I do not recall
But they are gone to early death, who late in school
Distinguished the belt feed lever from the belt holding pawl.

[87]

JAMES DICKEY

from *Drinking from a Helmet*

I

I climbed out, tired of waiting
For my foxhole to turn in the earth
On its side or its back for a grave,
And got in line
Somewhere in the roaring of dust.
Every tree on the island was nowhere,
Blasted away.

II

In the middle of combat, a graveyard
Was advancing after the troops
With laths and balls of string;
Grass already tinged it with order.
Between the new graves and the foxholes
A green water-truck stalled out.
I moved up on it, behind
The hill that cut off the firing.

III

My turn, and I shoved forward
A helmet I picked from the ground,
Not daring to take mine off
Where somebody else may have come
Loose from the steel of his head.

IV

Keeping the foxhole doubled
In my body and begging
For water, safety, and air,
I drew water out of the truckside
As if dreaming the helmet full.
In my hands, the sun
Came on in a feathery light.

In midair, water trimming
To my skinny dog-faced look
Showed my life's first all-out beard
Growing wildly, escaping from childhood,
Like the beards of the dead, all now
Underfoot beginning to grow.
Selected ripples wove through it,
Knocked loose with a touch from all sides
Of a brain killed early that morning,
Most likely, and now
In its absence holding
My sealed, sunny image from harm,
Weighing down my hands,
Shipping at the edges,
Too heavy on one side, then the other.

I drank, with the timing of rust.
A vast military wedding
Somewhere advanced one step.

. . .

Enough
Shining, I picked up my carbine and said.
I threw my old helmet down
And put the wet one on.
Warmed water ran over my face.
My last thought changed, and I knew
I inherited one of the dead.

I saw tremendous trees
That would grow on the sun if they could,
Towering. I saw a fence
And two boys facing each other,
Quietly talking,
Looking in at the gigantic redwoods,

The rings in the trunks turning slowly
To raise up stupendous green.
They went away, one turning
The wheels of a blue bicycle,
The smaller one curled catercornered
In the handlebar basket.

XVIII

I would survive and go there,
Stepping off the train in a helmet
That held a man's last thought,
Which showed him his older brother
Showing him trees.
I would ride through all
California upon two wheels
Until I came to the white
Dirt road where they had been,
Hoping to meet his blond brother,
And to walk with him into the wood
Until we were lost,
Then take off the helmet
And tell him where I had stood,
What poured, what spilled, what swallowed:

XIX

And tell him I was the man.

KEITH DOUGLAS

Vergissmeinnicht

Three weeks gone and the combatants gone
returning over the nightmare ground
we found the place again, and found
the soldier sprawling in the sun.

The frowning barrel of his gun
overshadowing. As we came on
that day, he hit my tank with one
like the entry of a demon.

Look. Here in the gunpit spoil
the dishonoured picture of his girl
who has put: *Steffi. Vergissmeinnicht*
in a copybook gothic script.

We see him almost with content,
abased, and seeming to have paid
and mocked at by his own equipment
that's hard and good when he's decayed.

But she would weep to see today
how on his skin the swart flies move;
the dust upon the paper eye
and the burst stomach like a cave.

For here the lover and killer are mingled
who had one body and one heart.
And death who had the soldier singled
has done the lover mortal hurt.

Tunisia 1943

JOHN CIARDI

Massive Retaliation

I gaped, admitted, at some of what we did
those days at skip-ocean, watching the shore towns blow
like spouts below us, staring into volcanoes
at the half-closed red eye under everything.

One moon-mist night six miles over Nagoya
we let our fish go, banked wide over mountains.
A searchlight from the world washed us in green,
lost us to black, returned, lost us again.

Those wars were all waiting. I waited, looking down
into the dark of one more thing set fire to.

Then we were over ocean and alive.
The blaze went out. We dove into the dawn.

It was as far from home as we could go.
I remember the teeth of the mountains of the moon
and the meteors falling in. By afternoon
it was official. Something had been done.

We acted boredom but lived better. Once,
above the sea, circling a rendezvous rock,
we filled the east and west with silver sharks
pinwheeling like a marriage race of gods.

It was a thousand of ourselves we saw.
A thousand theorems spiralled from the sun
to some proof statelier than the thing done.
A sky-wide silver coming of the law.

Even toward murder such possibility
meets and becomes. Like empires on their shields
we circle over time, and the great wheel
blazed like a reason over the lighted sea.

I gaped for all good men at what we were,
dressed in such bridals, spilling from the sun,
stuffed with such thunderbolts, and come
so far from home, almost beyond return.

Saipan 1944–5, aerial offensive against Japan

DAVID CAMPBELL

Men in Green

Oh, there were fifteen men in green,
 Each with a tommy-gun,
Who leapt into my plane at dawn;
 We rose to meet the sun.

We set our course towards the east
 And climbed into the day
Till the ribbed jungle underneath
 Like a giant fossil lay.

We climbed towards the distant range,
 Where two white paws of cloud
Clutched at the shoulders of the pass;
 The green men laughed aloud.

They did not fear the ape-like cloud
 That climbed the mountain crest
And hung from ropes invisible
 With lightning in its breast.

They did not fear the summer's sun
 In whose hot centre lie
A hundred hissing cannon shells
 For the unwatchful eye.

And when on Dobadura's field
 We landed, each man raised
His thumb towards the open sky;
 But to their right I gazed.

For fifteen men in jungle green
 Rose from the kunai grass
And came towards the plane. My men
 In silence watched them pass;
It seemed they looked upon themselves
 In Time's prophetic glass.

Oh, there were some leaned on a stick
 And some on stretchers lay,
But few walked on their own two feet
 In the early green of day.

(They did not heed the ape-like cloud
 That climbed the mountain crest;
They did not fear the summer's sun
 With bullets for their breast.)

Their eyes were bright, their looks were dull;
    Their skin had turned to clay.
Nature had met them in the night
    And stalked them in the day.

And I think still of men in green
    On the Soputa track,
With fifteen spitting tommy-guns
    To keep the jungle back.

PETER HUCHEL

Winter Billet

I sit by the shed,
Oiling my rifle:

A foraging hen
With her foot imprints
Lightly on snow
A script as old as the world,
A sign as old as the world,
Lightly on snow
The tree of life.

I know the butcher
And his way of killing.
I know the axe.
I know the chopping-block.

Across the shed
You will flutter,
Stump with no head,
Yet still a bird
That presses a twitching wing
Down on the split wood.

I know the butcher.
I sit by the shed,
Oiling my rifle.

translated by Michael Hamburger

DONALD M. WOODRUFF

Night Attack

The Dark Angel and I met as the long hand was vertical.
The barrage moved up with little mincing steps and we followed.
We crept forward through the Italian mud on our foreign bellies.
The flares made low constellations.

Then the Dark Angel touched the grenades at my belt, saying,
'Send these after me – I will be up ahead.'
I did as he bade.
We took the emplacement together.

EI YAMAGUCHI

The Setting Sun

We press forward
with our bayonets glinting in the setting sun.

Three girls, clasped hand in hand,
sink into the creek.

On the darkling ground
only we are left behind.

translated by Ichiro Kônô and Rikutaro Fukuda

RANDALL JARRELL

The Sick Nought

Do the wife and baby travelling to see
Your grey pajamas and sick worried face
Remind you of something, soldier? I remember
You convalescing washing plates, or mopping
The endless corridors your shoes had scuffed;
And in the crowded room you rubbed your cheek
Against your wife's thin elbow like a pony.
But you are something there are millions of.
How can I care about you much, or pick you out
From all the others other people loved
And sent away to die for them? You are a ticket
Someone bought and lost on, a stray animal:
You have lost even the right to be condemned.
I see you looking helplessly around, in histories,
Bewildered with your terrible companions, Pain
And Death and Empire: what have you understood, to die?
Were you worth, soldiers, all that people said
To be spent so willingly? Surely your one theory, to live,
Is nonsense to the practice of the centuries.
What is demanded in the trade of states
But lives, your lives? – the one commodity.

MIKLÓS RADNÓTI

The Second Eclogue

Pilot:
Last night we went far; in rage I laughed, I was so mad.
Their fighters were all droning like a bee-swarm overhead.
Their defence was strong and, friend, o how they fired and fired!
Till over the horizon our relief squadron appeared.
I just missed being shot down and scraped together below,
But see, I am back! And tomorrow, this craven Europe shall know

Fear in their air-raid shelters, as they tremble hidden away . . .
But enough of that, let's leave it. Have you written since yesterday?

Poet:
I have. The poet writes, as dogs howl or cats mew
Or small fish coyly spawn. What else am I to do?
I write about everything – write even for you, up there,
So that flying you may know of my life and of how I fare
When between the rows of houses, blown up and tumbling down,
The bloodshot light of the moon reels drunkenly around,
When the city squares bulge, all of them terror-stricken,
Breathing stops, and even the sky seems to sicken,
And the planes keep coming on, then disappear, and then
All swoop, like jabbering madness, down from the sky again!
I write; what else can I do? If you knew how dangerous
A poem can be, how frail, how capricious a single verse . . .
For that involves courage too – you see? Poets write,
Cats mew, dogs howl, small fish . . . and so on; but you who fight,
What do you know? Nothing. You listen, but all you hear
Is the plane you have just left droning on in your ear;
No use denying it, friend. It's become a part of you.
What do you think about as you fly above in the blue?

Pilot:
Laugh at me: I'm scared. And I long to lie in repose
On a bed beside my love, and for these eyes to close.
Or else, under my breath, I would softly hum her a tune
In the wild and steamy chaos of the flying-men's canteen.
Up there, I want to come down; down here, to be back in space:
In this world moulded for me, for me there is no place.
And, I know full well, I have grown too fond of my aeroplane,
True; but, when hit, the rhythm both suffer at is the same . . .
But you know and will write about it! It won't be a secret that I,
Who now just destroy, homeless between the earth and the sky,
Lived as a man lives. Alas, who'd understand or believe it?
Will you write of me?

Poet: If I live, if there's anyone left to read it.

27 April 1941

translated by Clive Wilmer and George Gömöri

[97]

KEITH DOUGLAS

How to Kill

Under the parabola of a ball,
a child turning into a man,
I looked into the air too long.
The ball fell in my hand, it sang
in the closed fist: *Open Open*
Behold a gift designed to kill.

Now in my dial of glass appears
the soldier who is going to die.
He smiles, and moves about in ways
his mother knows, habits of his.
The wires touch his face: I cry
NOW. Death, like a familiar, hears

and look, has made a man of dust
of a man of flesh. This sorcery
I do. Being damned, I am amused
to see the centre of love diffused
and the waves of love travel into vacancy.
How easy it is to make a ghost.

The weightless mosquito touches
her tiny shadow on the stone,
and with how like, how infinite
a lightness, man and shadow meet.
They fuse. A shadow is a man
when the mosquito death approaches.

Tunisia-Cairo, 1943

ERIC ROLLS

Dog Fight

Inside
The wireless is irritable with static.
The relieving sig. turns down the volume
And strains to hear his call sign.

Outside
The relieved sig. is relieving himself.
He is trying to piss his full name in the dust.
He has been saving up for hours.
He has to concentrate to control the flow.

Overhead
Two Zeros come out of cloud.
They hope to beat the Lightnings to the take off.

On the ground
The Lightnings are already rolling.
They have been forewarned.
The cloud was too far from the strip anyway.
One Zero turns and bolts.
The other climbs
To try to stop the Lightnings getting above him.

The sig. has finished his first Christian name neatly.
He takes two paces right and begins a capital W.

A morse signal offers an urgent weather report.
Two spotters jam each other in plain language
Reporting the Zeros
Which had already been reported.

The Lightnings are too fast for the Zero.
Only one goes in to attack.
It seems so easy:
There is a burst of smoke

And the Zero begins a slow spiral to ground.
It looks like a feather coming down.
You think about reaching up to catch it.

The sig. finds it harder near the end.
The pressure is dropping
And there is a T to be crossed.

The message about the Zeros
Has been relayed to Port Moresby
And the sig. has got down the coded weather report.
He is sending R for received.

There is another little burst of smoke
As the Zero hits the ground.
Two drops of urine
Make sufficient dent in the dust
To dot a final I.
A Morse signal sounds the end of transmission.

JAMES DICKEY

The Performance

The last time I saw Donald Armstrong
He was staggering oddly off into the sun,
Going down, of the Philippine Islands.
I let my shovel fall, and put that hand
Above my eyes, and moved some way to one side
That his body might pass through the sun,

And I saw how well he was not
Standing there on his hands,
On his spindle-shanked forearms balanced,
Unbalanced, with his big feet looming and waving
In the great, untrustworthy air
He flew in each night, when it darkened.

Dust fanned in scraped puffs from the earth
Between his arms, and blood turned his face inside
        out,
To demonstrate its suppleness
Of veins, as he perfected his role.
Next day, he toppled his head off
On an island beach to the south,

And the enemy's two-handed sword
Did not fall from anyone's hands
At that miraculous sight,
As the head rolled over upon
Its wide-eyed face, and fell
Into the inadequate grave

He had dug for himself, under pressure.
Yet I put my flat hand to my eyebrows
Months later, to see him again
In the sun, when I learned how he died,
And imagined him, there,
Come, judged, before his small captors,

Doing all his lean tricks to amaze them –
The back somersault, the kip-up –
And at last, the stand on his hands,
Perfect, with his feet together,
His head down, evenly breathing,
As the sun poured up from the sea

And the headsman broke down
In a blaze of tears, in that light
Of the thin, long human frame
Upside down in its own strange joy,
And, if some other one had not told him,
Would have cut off the feet

Instead of the head,
And if Armstrong had not presently risen
In kingly, round-shouldered attendance,

And then knelt down in himself
Beside his hacked, glittering grave, having done
All things in this life that he could.

C. D. GRIFFIN

Changi Impromptu

Fire in the clouds above the greying hill
Broad flames are blazoning the western sky,
With pageantries of sunset, soon to die
Into the birth of twilight; but alone
I must endure this grandeur. Oh my dear,
What wasted lavishness is here!

Black paper palms are strung across the moon,
Cheap theatre moon, whose stage scene light
Darkens the shadows of the back-drop night,
The orchestra of evening plays its tune,
The slender casuarinas softly blew
Faint whispers to the stars. The subtle flow
Of eastern perfume from the temple flowers
Carries messages of forgotten years,
And tears, my sweet, our tears.

Strong is emotion, but its powers seem spent.
New too, the sun of victory is set,
The halcyon dreams we had, our fears,
The rapture and the ecstasy of youth
Are dreams no longer, they are truth.
The spirit of mankind is stronger yet.
What walls has prison, when my thoughts are free
And soars to meet your love, your love for me!

RANDALL JARRELL

Eighth Air Force

If, in an odd angle of the hutment,
A puppy laps the water from a can
Of flowers, and the drunk sergeant shaving
Whistles O Paradiso! – shall I say that man
Is not as men have said: a wolf to man?

The other murderers troop in yawning;
Three of them play Pitch, one sleeps, and one
Lies counting missions, lies there sweating
Till even his heart beats: One; One; One.
O murderers! . . . Still, this is how it's done:

This is a war . . . But since these play, before they die,
Like puppies with their puppy; since, a man,
I did as these have done, but did not die –
I will content the people as I can
And give up these to them: Behold the man!

I have suffered, in a dream, because of him,
Many things; for this last saviour, man,
I have lied as I lie now. But what is lying?
Men wash their hands, in blood, as best they can:
I find no fault in this just man.

ALAN ROSS

Captain's Fur Collar

Stained and wet as shot rabbit
And his eye clinging to a thread
Like spit, a bullseye that might
Be swallowed whole, taking sight
With it.

Hiding his forehead
He picked his way from the bridge
With the indifference of a waiter.

We found him hours later,
Bolt upright on the edge
Of his bunk two decks below,
Eye dangling like a monocle, face like snow.

EVGENY VINOKUROV

I Don't Remember Him

I don't remember him.
I never saw him
In his Moscow flat,
Trying to catch hold of his braces
From behind, to fasten them
On to his trousers at the back.
I don't remember him in the quarantine station either,
As he stood naked in line,
Waiting for the handful of liquid coal-tar soap.
I don't remember him even
In that moment of shame,
When he forgot the word 'sling swivel',
And stared dumbly at the ground,
Under the frosty gaze of the sergeant.
I don't even remember
His terrible screaming . . .
All I remember are his two eyes,
Looking out from under half-closed lids,
When I cradled
The stumps of his legs,
To stop them banging against the boards
Inside the jolting truck.

translated by A. Rudolf and D. Weissbort

ANNA ŚWIRSZCZYŃSKA

Twenty of My Sons

In my ward
lie twenty soldiers' bellies.
Ripped open, bloody,
fighting fiercely
for life.

I know them all by heart,
by day I bring them bedpans, wash off the excrement.
By night I dream
that I bring them bedpans,
wash off the excrement.

When one of the bellies
dies in my dream
I wake with a start
and go up to the bed on tiptoe.

In my ward
fighting tooth and nail against nothingness are
twenty of my sons.

translated by Magnus Jan Krynski and Robert Macguire

RANDALL JARRELL

The Death of the Ball Turret Gunner

From my mother's sleep I fell into the State,
And I hunched in its belly till my wet fur froze.
Six miles from earth, loosed from its dream of life,
I woke to black flak and the nightmare fighters.
When I died they washed me out of the turret with a hose.

ODYSSEUS ELYTIS

from *Heroic and Elegiac Song for the Lost Second Lieutenant of the Albanian Campaign*

III

For those men night was a more bitter day
They melted iron, chewed the earth
Their God smelled of gunpowder and mule-hide

Each thunderclap was death riding the sky
Each thunderclap a man smiling in the face
Of death – let fate say what she will.

Suddenly the moment misfired and struck courage
Hurled splinters head-on into the sun
Binoculars, sights, mortars, froze with terror.

Easily, like calico that the wind rips
Easily, like lungs that stones have punctured
The helmet rolled to the left side . . .

For one moment only roots shook in the soil
Then the smoke dissolved and the day tried timidly
To beguile the infernal tumult.

But night rose up like a spurned viper
Death paused one second on the brink –
Then struck deeply with his pallid claws.

IV

Now with a still wind in his quiet hair
A twig of forgetfulness at his left ear
He lies on the scorched cape
Like a garden the birds have suddenly deserted
Like a song gagged in the darkness
Like an angel's watch that has stopped

Eyelashes barely whispered goodbye
And bewilderment became rigid ...

He lies on the scorched cape
Black ages round him
Bay at the terrible silence with dogs' skeletons
And hours that have once more turned into stone pigeons
Listen attentively:
But laughter is burnt, earth has grown deaf,
No one heard that last, that final cry
The whole world emptied with that very last cry
Beneath the five cedars
Without other candles
He lies on the scorched cape.
The helmet is empty, the blood full of dirt,
At his side the arm half shot away
And between the eyebrows –
Small bitter red-black spring
Spring whose memory freezes.

O do not look O do not look at the place where life
Where life has left him. Do not say how the smoke of dawn has
Do not say how the smoke of dawn has risen
This is the way one moment this is the way
This is the way one moment deserts the other
And this is the way the all-powerful suddenly deserts the world.

translated by Edmund Keeley and Peter Sherrard

R. N. CURREY

Unseen Fire

This is a damned inhuman sort of war.
I have been fighting in a dressing-gown
Most of the night; I cannot see the guns,
The sweating gun-detachments or the planes;

I sweat down here before a symbol thrown
Upon a screen, sift facts, initiate
Swift calculations and swift orders; wait
For the precise split-second to order fire.

We chant our ritual words; beyond the phones
A ghost repeats the orders to the guns:
One Fire . . . Two Fire . . . ghosts answer: the guns roar
Abruptly; and an aircraft waging war
Inhumanly from nearly five miles height
Meets our bouquet of death – and turns sharp right.

GEOFFREY HOLLOWAY

Rhine Jump, 1944

They dropped us on the guns, left us in a flaring
lurch of slipstream kicking like sprayed flies, –
till canopies shook sudden heads, inhaled, held a breath, –
alive again we slanted down,
too many, into their doomed sights.

One scrambled moment it was red, green,
dragging to the door of the Douglas then
falling through a monstrous aviary roof
on Guy Fawkes Night (only this was day)
into shrill scarifying glory . . .

then Germany, the Fatherland, a zooming field –
banged down on it, stood up among the chaos, with
fingers flopped like rubber gloves trying
to slap one's box, slough the afterbirth of chute,
make somehow that snatch of wood.

There were chutes already in those trees, caught:
battalion boys who'd dropped too late or drifted . . .
harness-ravelled, cocooned there –
like silkworms, moveless, wet . . .
so easy, against all that white.

[108]

But not so many resistive earthworms –
the early birds had seen to that.
Soon, it was rendezvous: a stodgy farm.
The war was folding: fight-thin.
Prisoners happened; columned, toneless.

Next day it was hearing tales again,
having a kip in a pigsty, scouting the dropping-zone
to get silk (knickers for sweethearts, wives);
maybe a green envelope, speculation
about leave, Japan.

Oh and a gun-pit by the way, an 88:
bodiless, nothing special, –
only the pro's interest in other's kit:
grey slacks for the use of, old, ersatz;
with a brown inside stripe: non-ersatz.

DENIS GLOVER

Burial at Sea, off France

Airman, your eager spirit fled,
Too long you rolled in the tide
Unheedingly, unheeded, now not wedded
To those bright wings, now dead;

Taking the sodden papers from your side
What could we do more, with clumsy prayer,
Than give you again to the deep
In which you died?

Burying you we saw the lives that each
In plane, ship, tank or landing craft
Hoped to preserve yet thrust
Numberless, nameless, to the desperate beach,

Necessity compelling. But loss
Even of the ultimate breath
And body of being meant more
Than sad wreckage the waves tossed:

You, airman, from the cloud
Spinning on that last sortie
Played your unwished-for part,
Making our triumph less proud.

RANDALL JARRELL

Losses

It was not dying: everybody died.
It was not dying: we had died before
In the routine crashes – and our fields
Called up the papers, wrote home to our folks,
And the rates rose, all because of us.
We died on the wrong page of the almanac,
Scattered on mountains fifty miles away;
Diving on haystacks, fighting with a friend,
We blazed up on the lines we never saw.
We died like aunts or pets or foreigners.
(When we left high school nothing else had died
For us to figure we had died like.)

In our new planes, with our new crews, we bombed
The ranges by the desert or the shore,
Fired at towed targets, waited for our scores –
And turned into replacements and woke up
One morning, over England, operational.
It wasn't different: but if we died
It was not an accident but a mistake
(But an easy one for anyone to make).
We read our mail and counted up our missions –
In bombers named for girls, we burned
The cities we had learned about in school –

Till our lives wore out; our bodies lay among
The people we had killed and never seen.
When we lasted long enough they gave us medals;
When we died they said, 'Our casualties were low'.
They said, 'Here are the maps'; we burned the cities.

It was not dying – no, not ever dying;
But the night I died I dreamed that I was dead,
And the cities said to me: 'Why are you dying?
We are satisfied, if you are; but why did I die?'

VERNON SCANNELL

War Graves at El Alamein

When they were little children they explored
Forests dense with dangers, were pursued
By beast, or giant wielding knife or sword
And terrified they found their feet were glued
Firmly to the ground; they could not scream
Or run, yet they were never stabbed or gored
But always woke to find it just a dream.

Years and nightmares later they became
Old enough to put on uniform,
And in parched throats they gagged upon the same
Taste of childhood terror in a storm
Of killing thunder they must battle through.
Now, unimportant pieces in the game,
They sleep and know that last bad dream was true.

RUDOLF LANGER

Wounded No Doubt and Pale from Battle

In ancient books
I saw him prostrate
with his shield and here
on the spot,
wounded no doubt and pale
from battle, ultimately
with small head raised
uttering the truth
of it all.

The fear in the eye sockets
moves us more than the sadness
which later sits down on the edge
and laments what has happened.
Or else the joy of killing
might forever be greater than either
and the prostrate man here
sees the fatal blow coming
and fixes it in terror.

Before a bronze sculpture by Henry Moore
in the imperial palace at Goslar, 1976

translated by Ewald Osers

V

'*At night and in the wind
and the rain*'

ALUN LEWIS

Song (On seeing dead bodies floating off the Cape)

The first month of his absence
I was numb and sick
And where he'd left his promise
Life did not turn or kick.
The seed, the seed of love was sick.

The second month my eyes were sunk
In the darkness of despair,
And my bed was like a grave
And his ghost was lying there.
And my heart was sick with care.

The third month of his going
I thought I heard him say
'Our course deflected slightly
On the thirty-second day –'
The tempest blew his words away.

And he was lost among the waves,
The ship rolled helpless in the sea,
The fourth month of his voyage
He shouted grievously
'Beloved, do not think of me.'

The flying fish like kingfishers
Skim the sea's bewildered crests,
The whales blow steaming fountains,
The sea-gulls have no nests
Where my lover sways and rests.

We never thought to buy or sell
The life that blooms or withers in the leaf,
And I'll not stir, so he sleeps well,
Though cell by cell the coral reef
Builds an eternity of grief.

[115]

But oh! the drag and dullness of my Self;
The turning seasons wither in my head;
All this slowness, all this hardness,
The nearness that is waiting in my bed,
The gradual self-effacement of the dead.

KENNETH SLESSOR

Beach Burial

Softly and humbly to the Gulf of Arabs
The convoys of dead sailors come;
At night they sway and wander in the waters far under,
But morning rolls them in the foam.

Between the sob and clubbing of the gunfire
Someone, it seems, has time for this,
To pluck them from the shallows and bury them in burrows
And tread the sand upon their nakedness;

And each cross, the driven stake of tidewood,
Bears the last signature of men,
Written with such perplexity, with such bewildered pity,
The words choke as they begin –

'Unknown seaman' – the ghostly pencil
Wavers and fades, the purple drips,
The breath of the wet season has washed their inscriptions
As blue as drowned men's lips,

Dead seamen, gone in search of the same landfall,
Whether as enemies they fought,
Or fought with us, or neither; the sand joins them together,
Enlisted on the other front.

El Alamein

Enfidaville

In the church fallen like dancers
lie the Virgin and St. Therese
on little pillows of dust.
The detonations of the last few days
tore down the ornamental plasters
shivered the hands of Christ.

The men and women who moved like candles
in and out of the houses and the streets
are all gone. The white houses are bare
black cages. No one is left to greet
the ghosts tugging at doorhandles
opening doors that are not there.

Now the daylight coming in from the fields
like a labourer, tired and sad,
is peering about among the wreckage, goes
past some corners as though with averted head
not looking at the pain this town holds,
seeing no one move behind the windows.

But already they are coming back; to search
like ants, poking in the debris, finding in it
a bed or a piano and carrying it out.
Who would not love them at this minute?
I seem again to meet
the blue eyes of the images in the church.

Tunisia, May 1943

BERTOLT BRECHT

1940

I

Spring is coming. The gentle winds
Are freeing the cliffs of their winter ice.
Trembling, the peoples of the north await
The battle fleets of the house-painter.

II

Out of the libraries
Emerge the butchers.
Pressing their children closer
Mothers stand and humbly search
The skies for the inventions of learned men.

III

The designers sit
Hunched in the drawing offices:
One wrong figure, and the enemy's cities
Will remain undestroyed.

IV

Fog envelops
The road
The poplars
The farms and
The artillery.

V

I am now living on the small island of Lidingo.
But one night recently
I had heavy dreams and I dreamed I was in a city
And discovered that its street signs
Were in German. I awoke
Bathed in sweat, saw the fir tree
Black as night before my window, and realised with relief:
I was in a foreign land.

VI

My young son asks me: Should I learn mathematics?
What for, I'm inclined to say. That two bits of bread are more than
      one
You'll notice anyway.
My young son asks me: Should I learn French?
What for, I'm inclined to say. That empire is going under.
Just rub your hand across your belly and groan
And you'll be understood all right.
My young son asks me: should I learn history?
What for, I'm inclined to say. Learn to stick your head in the ground
Then maybe you'll come through.

Yes, learn mathematics, I tell him
Learn French, learn history!

VII

In front of the whitewashed wall
Stands the black military case with the manuscripts.
On it lie the smoking things with the copper ashtrays.
The Chinese scroll depicting the Doubter
Hangs above it. The masks are there too. And by the bedstead
Stands the little six-valve radio.
Mornings
I turn it on and hear
The victory bulletins of my enemies.

VIII

Fleeing from my fellow-countrymen
I have now reached Finland. Friends
Whom yesterday I didn't know, put up some beds
In clean rooms. Over the radio
I hear the victory bulletins of the scum of the earth.
   Curiously
I examine a map of the continent. High up in Lapland
Towards the Arctic Ocean
I can still see a small door.

translated by Sammy McLean

KRZYSZTOF KAMIL BACZYŃSKI

Evil Lullaby

Autumn leaves, the smell of your hair,
the cracked clock of fear clatters.
Chill breath blows from the stars,
summer's candles gutter out
                          and my grief
runs into your arms each evening like a black dog.

Can you sleep? A dead and weeping alder tree
is howling long into the night – a dome of echoes.
We are sailing, no ports, no haven shell for us,
you know it: sadness – the lurking patrol – just waiting.
The good fairytale dragon is now a dream turned to stone,
a ghost dream – night passes, a monument touching Heaven.
Only the shriek of a spectre, peasant pitchfork-pierced,
only the shriek of a moon-strangled cat.
Can you sleep? Today a mad poet
hanged himself in the dark clamour of isolated pines,
and the rain dragged a waxwork corpse, to the wind's flutes,
for ages through the streets by the hair.

Sleep,
it is quiet.
The night swells against the panes
and the wind blind like me kneels outside the house.
Who wrenched that carefree time from us –
my love?

10/11 September, night, 1940

translated by Anna Zukowska-Wilcocks and Richard Wilcocks

KRZYSZTOF KAMIL BACZYŃSKI

A Generation (Winter 1941)

They froze to fingers – strings
of a thin shriek of plants.
One is reared for the coffin
which is how this present time reared us.

Rivers of fire stood still
clad with crimson floes:
at night a dream like a burning torch
haunts with a severed head.

What else do you? In a frost
the world is loose sawdust.
Eyes hard as stones.
It is the snow, not the heart creaking.

All of you – you are a frozen column
on the grave of your own songs –
what else do you?
It is death, not threads of light.

Grains of salt from Heaven?
Tears become part of a face of flint?
Does earth mature as painfully
as the way this present time reared us?

November 1941

translated by Anna Zukowska-Wilcocks and Richard Wilcocks

IMRE CSNÁDI

Silent Prayer of Peasants

Lord, it's very hard to get
your politics, try as we may.
Bad times – you can see it yet.
That world war that came our way,
crisis and such we had to shoulder –
you know it seemed at times we'd rather
snuff it than go on. Made us bolder
in rapping your saints, you too, father.

What would your reaction be right now
if you were in the room with us, to watch
the showers that have been pouring down
like nemesis, our whole summer awash?

Look at our hay rotting in clumps,
our meadow utterly rained away
in floodwater. The cow lows at us:
what will she chew in winter? clay?

Frogs are croaking through our wheatfields,
reeds and waterplants make merry . . .
And what's the future of this story?
We don't know what tomorrow yields!

But you are not our only Lord –
we're in the slobbery ravenous jaws
of other lords that never pause
in their 'more! more! you can afford
taxes! taxes!' – They ask, they get;
add fret and fever to fever and fret.

Your Four Horsemen gallop and neigh.
The four corners of heaven shake.
Night-watchmen drive dogs mad, and take
the call-up papers for next day.

translated by Edwin Morgan 1941

RACHEL KORN

A Letter from Uzbekistan

My friend beyond the distant seas
this letter is for you –
it's March in the land of Uzbekistan
when the almond tree and the apricot bloom
in every ditch, beside every wall,
but where can I find words to make you understand?
My hand is tired, the skin is stiff,
it pulls away like an empty sack,
and my greatest dream is
a loaf of bread.

When I left the house
a dead dog
lay facing the door,
the spring breeze
stirred his ragged fur

and just then a wagon passed,
a white coffin slanting over the wheel.
A shrivelled *babke* stopped
and crossed herself with a dry hand
slowly and for a long time.

'The hunger, the hunger is in the land again –
he played with their child yesterday,
I know him, I know him, he's my neighbor's dog.
And look at the size of the coffin,
if we had that for beds, tables, benches –
God help us, do you think the one in the white box
died of sickness?
It's hunger, hunger in the land.

And you, dove, show me your hand –
How long do you think you'll be walking the earth?
I see your step already weighted with death.'

[123]

The sun shone bright,
I stood still
and listened.

But I meant to write you a letter, my friend –
do you recall my wild joy
in early spring
when the earth smelled of fresh grass
and my lips like buds on a tree
filled with yearning
and flowering dream,
do you recall, my friend?

And today –
I want to crawl away into a hole
like an animal that senses the hour of her death is near,
and still my greatest dream is
at least a *slice* of bread

Fergana, March 1942

translated by Seymour Levitan

MIKLÓS RADNÓTI

The Fifth Eclogue

IN MEMORY OF GYORGY BALINT
[*fragment*]

My dear friend, how the cold of this poem made me shiver,
How afraid I was of words. Today too, I have fled it.
Have scribbled half-lines.
              I tried to write about something – about
Anything else, but in vain! This furtive night of terror
Admonishes: 'Speak of him'.
              And I start up, but the voice
Is silent again – like the dead, out there on Ukrainian fields.
You're missing.
          And autumn's brought no news of you. Again,

Through the forest, wild prophecy of winter is soughing;
    clouds fly
Heavy across the sky – till, snow-laden, they stop.
Alive still? Who knows?
                    Now *I* don't, nor do I fly into rage
When people shake their heads or in pain hide their faces.
And they know nothing.
                  But are you alive? Or only wounded?
Are you walking through fallen leaves and the odour of forest mud,
Or are you yourself but a fragrance?
                      Snow flutters over the fields.
'Missing' – the news thuds home.
                And my heart thumps once, then freezes.
At such times, between two of my ribs there's a bad pain that tenses
And throbs, your words said long ago now live so clearly
In my mind, and I feel your bodily presence as vividly
As if you were dead . . .
           Still, I can't write of you today!

21 November 1943

translated by Clive Wilmer and George Gömöri

ANGELOS SIKELIANOS

Agraphon

Once at sunset Jesus and His disciples
were on the road outside the walls of Zion
when suddenly they came to where the town
for years had dumped its garbage: burnt mattresses
from sickbeds, broken pots, rags, filth.

And there, crowning the highest pile, its legs
pointing at the sky, lay a dog's bloated carcass;
and as the crows that covered it flew off
when they heard the approaching footsteps, such a stench
rose up from it that the disciples, hands
cupped over their nostrils, drew back as one man.

[125]

But Jesus calmly walked on by Himself
toward the pile, stood there, and then gazed
so closely at the carcass that one disciple,
not able to stop himself, called out from a distance,
'Rabbi, don't you smell that terrible stench?
How can you go on standing there?'

Jesus, His eyes fixed on the carcass,
answered: 'If your breath is pure, you'll smell
the same stench inside the town behind us.
But now my soul marvels at something else,
marvels at what comes out of this corruption.
Look how the dog's teeth glitter in the sun:
like hailstones, like a lily, beyond decay,
a great pledge, mirror of the Eternal, but also,
the harsh lightning flash, the hope of Justice!'
So He spoke; and whether or not the disciples
understood His words, they followed Him
as He moved on, silent.

                 'And now, Lord, I,
the very least of men, stand before you
and ponder those words, one thought in my mind:
give me, as now I walk outside this Zion,
and the world from end to end is all ruins, garbage,
all unburied corpses choking the sacred
springs of breath, inside and outside the city:
give me, Lord, as I walk through this terrible stench,
one single moment of Your holy calm,
so that I, dispassionate, may also pause
among this carrion and with my own eyes
somewhere see a token, white as hailstones,
as the lily – something glittering suddenly
deep inside me, above the putrefaction,
beyond the world's decay, like the dog's teeth
at which, Lord, that sunset You gazed in wonder:
a great pledge, mirror of the Eternal, but also
the harsh lightning-flash, the hope of Justice!'

translated by Edmund Keeley and Peter Sherrard

[126]

RENÉ CHAR

Freedom

It came along this white line that might signify dawn's emergence as well as death's candlestick.

It passed beyond the unconscious strands; it passed beyond the eviscerated summits.

They were ending: the cowardly-countenanced renunciation, the holiness of lying, the raw spirits of the executioner.

Its word was not a blind battering-ram but rather the canvas where my breath was inscribed.

With a pace unsure only behind absence, it came, a swan on the wound, along this white line.

translated by Denis Devlin and Jackson Mathews

JOHANNES BOBROWSKI

Kaunas 1941

Town,
branches over the river,
copper-coloured, like branching candles.
The banks call from the deep.
Then the lame girl
walked before dusk,
her skirt of darkest red.

And I know the steps,
the slope, this house. There is no
fire. Under this roof
lives the Jewess, lives whispering
in the Jews' silence
– the faces of the daughters
a white water. Noisily
the murderers pass the gate. We walk
softly, in musty air, in the track of wolves.

[127]

At evening we looked out
over a stony valley. The hawk
swept round the broad dome.
We saw the old town, house after house
running down to the river.

Will you walk over
the hill? The grey processions
– old men and sometimes boys –
die there. They walk
up the slope ahead of the slavering wolves.

Did my eyes avoid yours
brother? Sleep struck us
at the bloody wall. So we went on
blind to everything. We looked
like gipsies at the villages
in the oakwood, the summer
snow on the roofs.

I shall walk on the stone banks
under the rainy bushes,
listen in the haze of the plains.
There were swallows upstream
and the woodpigeon called
in the green night:
My dark is already come.

translated by Ruth and Matthew Mead

EUGENIO MONTALE

Hitler Spring

Né quella ch'a verder lo sol si gira . . .
DANTE (?) *a* GIOVANNI QUIRINI

Dense the white cloud of the moths going mad
whirls about faint globes and on the embankment,

stretches along the ground a coverlet on which
the foot crackles as on sugar; the coming summer frees
the nightly chill that till now was enclosed
in the secret pits of the dead season,
in orchards that from Maiano clamber down to these sands.

No time ago along the thoroughfare shot a hellish messenger
amid the chant-chanting of henchmen, a mystic gulf lit
and hung with hooked crosses caught and swallowed him,
the shop windows are closed, poor
and harmless though they too are armed
with cannons and toys of war,
the butcher has closed his shutters – he would take berries
and decorate the heads of slaughtered kids,
the rite of mild executioners who do not yet know blood
has turned to a foul reeling of shattered wings,
of wraiths at the river-edge, and the water goes on gnawing
the banks and no one now is guiltless.

All for nothing, then? – and the Roman
candles at San Giovanni whitening
the horizon slowly, and the pledges and the long
farewells strong as vows, in the stricken waiting
for the horde (but a gem streaked the air and trickled
upon the ice-pack, and the coastline of your shores
the angels of Tobias, the seven, the seed
of the future) and the heliotropes born

from out your hands – all burnt and sucked dry
by a pollen that hisses like fire
and is toothed like the blizzard . . .
                                    O the wounded
springtime is still holiday if it freezes
this death of ours in death! Look up again,
up high, it is your fate, Clizia, you
who, changed, still harbour that unchanged love,
until the blind sun you bear in you
dazzles in the Other and is destroyed
in Him, for everyone. Perhaps the sirens, the rising wail
that greets the monsters in the nightfall

of their witches' sabbath is already mingling
with the sound that loosed from heaven, descends, wins –
with the breathing of a dawn that tomorrow for everyone
may show again, white but without wings
of horror, on burnt wadis of the south . . .

translated by George Kay

LOUIS ARAGON

Tapestry of the Great Fear

This landscape masterpiece of modern terror
Has sharks and sirens, flying fish and swordfish
And hydra-headed birds like Lerna's hydra
What are they writing, white on blue in the sky?
Skimmers of earth, steel birds that stitch the air
To the stone houses, strident comet-birds
Enormous wasps like acrobatic matchsticks
That deck the flaming walls with primroses
Or flights of pink flamingoes in the sun
Kermesse in Flanders, witches at their Sabbath
On a broomstick the Messerschmitt rides down
Darkness at noon, night of the new Walpurgis
Apocalyptic time. Space where fear passes
With all its baggage train of tears and trembling
Do you recognise the fields, the birds of prey?
The steeple where the bells will never ring
The farm carts draped with bedclothes. A tame bear
A shawl. A dead man dropped like an old shoe
Hands clutching the torn belly. A grandfather's clock
Roaming herds of cattle, carcases, cries
Art bronzes by the roadside. Where will you sleep?
Children perched on the shoulders of strange men
Tramping off somewhere, while the gold of the barns
Gleams in their hair. Ditches where terror sits
The dying man in a cart who keeps asking
For herb tea, and complains of a cold sweat
A hunchbacked woman with a wedding dress
A birdcage that passed safely through the flames

A sewing machine. An old man. I can't walk
Just a step more. No let him die here, Marie
Evening soars down with silent wingbeats, joining
A velvet Brueghel to this Brueghel of hell.

translated by Malcolm Cowley

PIERRE JEAN-JOUVE
Untitled

They are not the blue mountains any more
Lebanon of my soul
Where is the beloved whose breasts are fawns
The lovers' chase
But death and ruin have usurped their place

Blind with noon
I thought only of those beloved fawns
And I sought daylight; yet the thunder
Fell by night from great angelic hands
Around criminals who were not struck down.

translated by Keith Bosley

MIROSLAV HOLUB
Five Minutes after the Air Raid

In Pilsen,
twenty-six Station Road,
she climbed to the third floor
up stairs which were all that was left
of the whole house,
she opened her door
full on to the sky,
stood gaping over the edge.

For this was the place
the world ended.

Then
she locked up carefully
lest someone steal
Sirius
or Aldebaran
from her kitchen,
went back downstairs
and settled herself
to wait
for the house to rise again
and for her husband to rise from the ashes
and for her children's hands and feet to be stuck back in place.

In the morning they found her
still as stone,
sparrows pecking her hands.

translated by George Theiner

KRZYSZTOF KAMIL BACZYŃSKI

The Rains

Rain like grey stalks, ashen pouring,
at the windows agony and grief.
I love rain like this, a rustle of strings,
rain – the pity of life.

Faraway trains travel yet further
without you. What? Without you. What?
into gardens of water, into lakes of sorrow,
into leaves, into avenues of glass roses.

Are you still waiting? Waiting still?
Rain is like compassion – it will wipe out everything:
blood from the battlefield, a man,
the air petrified with fear.

And still you are dreaming at the windows,
a mournful tombstone. Time's inscription

streams down its grim, deaf face
perhaps in rain, perhaps tears.

There, a love not really loving,
there, a blow not really painful,
but dark like the shriek of some bird,
there, the crying-out of flesh.

There, trespasses not coming back,
sometimes calling one to the other,
and there, as if at the great doors of a church,
you had a vision like a solitary dream.

Standing in the glassy rustling,
I feel the land drifting into the downpour.
All the beloved shall pass away,
first one, then all – bearing crosses,
yet others removed by the rain,
yet others vanished in the gloom,
they shall stand on the other side of the glass,
     as if made of steel,
and unseasoned, they shall pass by, pass by.

And the rains shall cease, shall slice
like scythes silent and painful,
and a shadow shall envelop, a shadow shall cleanse.
And loving, fighting, pleading like this
I shall stand at the source – the dark wells,
lifting my arms in a menacing silence,
like a dog under an empty voice's lash.

Unloved, unslain,
unfulfilled, signifying nothing,
I feel the rain or a cry from the heart,
everything to God in vain.
I shall be alone. Alone with darkness.
Only the teardrops, the rains, the rains
quieter and quieter, painless.

finished 21 February 1943
translated by Anna Zukowska-Wilocks and Richard Wilcocks

CHAIM GRADE

Refugees

1

At night and in the wind and the rain,
we're whirled on the roads,
in the parks, on steps and stations,
like masses of leaves.
And changing from train to train
we're already jealous
of those who don't have to beg for a drop of water:
God's already provided them
with a stone cushion.
And we're starving, and shaggy, a herd
of panicky animals,
fighting each other for a place on the soup line
with fists and hell-cries,
we want to split the skies
with our curses,
our eyes shining like knives,
we break out of a corner
to be whirled on the roads
at night, in the wind and the rain.

2

Famished wolves howl,
and the sons of Poland
have beards like overgrown swampgrass.
Like terrified oxen
tearing out of the slaughterhouse,
we ran from Lithuania.
And the Ukraine drove us out
from under their roofs
like screaming ravens.
Now the villages stoop and totter:
they, too, will lose
their homes in this storm.

3

The Nieman spat stones,
and the Don won't exactly rock us to sleep.
We kick up a dark cloud
that stretches from Minsk to the cold Samara.
Vilna ran into Zhitomir
and they fell
on top of each other, and broke
into sobs, both broken
on the roads of Siberia.
We've ripped through all the fences
between Europe and Asia,
and now we can hope
for only one thing: to poison
heaven with our injuries.
Oh, who will demand an accounting
for flesh
that becomes garbage on the roads
at night and in the wind and rain.

translated by Marc Kaminsky

RACHEL KORN

To My Daughter

When I led you out, the earth spurted blood and terror
with every step we took,
the greatest good was sudden death,
and a mother's blessing – the sure mercy of a bullet for her child.

The flowering acacias went the heavy way of exile
with the sky and us,
the air was burdened with their scent,
breathless, sweet, stifling in tears.

I wasn't brave enough to look back,
and when I saw my home and my mother's face in dreams,
I went grey.
My eyes are dry, but all my steps are tears.

How many lives are left to pray for?
How many graves am I closer to the earth?
What door will take me in
and where am I destined to fall?

You and I – the only two left of all our kin,
and I entrusted your young life to a star,
as my mother entrusted her quiet prayer,
my grandmother her burning tears, to God.

Only you and I – and if I don't make it through,
my mother's prayer is crying in your blood.
The call of all those generations is ripening in you,
our village path is waiting for your step.

Moscow, 1944
translated by Seymour Levitan

JÁNOS PILINSKY

Harbach 1944

At all times I see them.
The moon brilliant. A black shaft looms up.
Beneath it, harnessed men
haul an immense cart.

Dragging that giant wagon
which grows bigger as the night grows
their bodies are divided among
the dust, their hunger and their trembling.

They are carrying the road, they are carrying the land,
the bleak potato fields,
and all they know is the weight of everything,
the burden of the skylines

and the falling bodies of their companions
which almost grow into their own

as they lurch, living layers,
treading each other's footsteps.

The villages stay clear of them,
the gateways withdraw.
The distance, that has come to meet them,
reels away back.

Staggering, they wade knee deep
in the low, darkly-muffled clatter
of their wooden clogs
as through invisible leaf litter.

Already their bodies belong to silence.
And they thrust their faces towards the height
as if they strained for a scent
of the faraway celestial troughs

because, prepared for their coming
like an opened cattle-yard,
its gates flung savagely back,
death gapes to its hinges.

translated by Ted Hughes and Janos Csokits

EARLE BIRNEY

The Road to Nijmegen*

December my dear on the road to Nijmegen
between the stones and the bitten sky
was your face

Not yours at first
but only the countenance of lank canals
and gathered stares
(too rapt to note my passing)
of graves with frosted billy-tins for epitaphs
bones of tanks beside the stoven bridges

and old men in the mist
hacking the last chips
from a boulevard of stumps

These for miles and the fangs of homes
where women wheeled in the wind
on the tireless rims of their cycles
like tattered sailboats,
tossing over the cobbles

and the children
groping in gravel for knobs of coal
or clustered like wintered flies
at the back of mess huts
their legs standing like dead stems out of their clogs

Numbed on the long road to mangled Nijmegen
I thought that only the living of others assures us
the gentle and true we remember as trees walking
Their arms reach down from the light of kindness
into this Lazarus tomb

So peering through sleet as we neared Nijmegen
I glimpsed the rainbow arch of your eyes
Over the clank of the jeep
your quick grave laughter
outrising at last the rockets
brought me what spells I repeat
as I travel this road
that arrives at no future
and what creed I can bring
to our daily crimes
to this guilt
in the griefs of the old
and the graves of the young

*Nijmegen was in 1944–5 the town at the tip of the Canadian salient in Holland,
connected with rearward troops by a single much-bombed highway. The area had been
the scene of tank battles, artillery duels, air raids, buzz-bomb and V-2 rocket attacks. It
had also been denuded of trees, coal and foodstocks by the retreating Germans. The
winter was in all Europe one of the coldest of the century.

NIKOLA VAPTSAROV

Two Poems

Farewell

TO MY WIFE

Sometimes I'll come and see you in your sleep,
an unexpected far-off visitor.
Don't leave me standing outside in the street –
Don't bolt your door.

I'll enter softly, silently sit down
and force my gaze into the dark to see you.
And when my eyes have gazed their fill
I'll kiss you and I'll leave you.

• • •

The fight is merciless and fierce.
The fight is, as they put it, epic.
I fell. Another takes my place.
What does the individual matter?

The firing squad – and then the worms.
All this is logical enough.
But in the storm we'll be with you,
my people, you whom we have loved!

translated by Ewald Osers

ANNA ŚWIRSZCZYŃSKA

Building the Barricade

We were afraid as we built the barricade
under fire

The tavern-keeper, the jeweller's mistress, the barber,
all of us cowards.

[139]

The servant-girl fell to the ground
as she lugged a paving stone, we were terribly afraid
all of us cowards –
the janitor, the market-woman, the pensioner.

The pharmacist fell to the ground
as he dragged the door of a toilet,
we were even more afraid, the smuggler-woman,
the dressmaker, the streetcar driver,
all of us cowards.

A kid from reform school fell
as he dragged a sandbag,
you see we were really
afraid.

Though no one forced us,
we did build the barricade
under fire.

translated by Magnus Jan Krynski and Robert Maguire

ABRAHAM SUTZKEVER

*The Lead Plates at the Rom Press**

Arrayed at night, like fingers stretched through bars
To clutch the lit air of freedom,
We made for the press plates, to seize
The lead plates at the Rom printing works.
We were dreamers, we had to be soldiers,
And melt down, for our bullets, the spirit of the lead.

---

*The Rom Press since the end of the eighteenth century was a prestigious traditional press and publishing house in Vilna, later run by the Widow Rom and Sons. It was renowned for its editions of the Talmud as well as for promoting works of modern Yiddish and Hebrew literature. This poem is based on a projected plan of the Jewish underground to use the lead of the printing plates for ammunition to stock its tiny arsenal. The poem's images link the ghetto struggle with the ancient battles for Jerusalem before the fall of the Temple.

At some timeless native lair
We unlocked the seal once more.
Shrouded in shadow, by the glow of a lamp,
Like Temple ancients dipping oil
Into candelabrums of festal gold,
So, pouring out line after lettered line, did we.

Letter by melting letter the lead,
Liquefied bullets, gleamed with thoughts:
A verse from Babylon, a verse from Poland,
Seething, flowing into the one mold.
Now must Jewish grit, long concealed in words,
Detonate the world in a shot!

Who in Vilna Ghetto has beheld the hands
Of Jewish heroes clasping weapons
Has beheld Jerusalem in its throes,
The crumbling of those granite walls;
Grasping the words smelted into lead,
Conning their sounds by heart.

Vilna Ghetto, 12 September 1943
translated by Neal Kozodoy

EDVARD KOCBEK

The Game

I hold a chipped bowl in my hands
and wait in the camp kitchen queue.
And when I glance forward and back
I am shocked by a marvellous insight –
only now do we see ourselves right.
Someone has changed and revealed us,
as though shuffling a pack of cards,
cheekily, naughtily, rarely,
but above all, as in all games,
the odds are mysteriously even
and he has summoned our secret truth.

He that burrowed now walks upon air,
he that declaimed speeches now stammers in his dreams,
he who slept upon straw now commands the brigade
and the quiet woodcutter is full of questions;
he that quoted Homer is building bunkers
and he that ate in Paris is shaping a spoon;
the drinker licks the dew, the singer harkens to the silence,
the sexton sows mines, the miser collects wounds,
the farmhand is a stargazer, the coward a commando,
the poet a mule driver, the dreamer a telegraphist
and the local Casanova a trusty guide.

I hold a chipped bowl in my hands
and I look to my front and look back
and I can't stop looking at images,
a procession of ghosts, spirits on pilgrimage,
the winking of truths, the revelation of fates.
Someone has changed and defined us,
as though shuffling a pack of cards,
cheekily, naughtily, rarely.
And then I see myself at last
and reèl under the weight of dreams –
all are within me, as in a young mother.

translated by Michael Scammell and Veno Taufer

ANNA AKHMATOVA

from *Wind of War*

1. OATH

May she who says farewell to her dear one today,
convert her pain into strength.
We swear to our children, swear to the graves,
that no one will force us to submit!

[Leningrad, July 1941]

2. 'THEY SAID DRAMATIC GOODBYES'

They said dramatic goodbyes to their girlfriends,
and dressed up in new uniforms,
they kissed their mothers as they marched
away to play toy soldiers.
Not bad or good or mediocre,
they were all at their posts,
where no one is first or last . . .
They all went to their eternal rest.

[1943]

5. COURAGE

We know what now lies in the balance
and what is coming to pass.
Courage's hour has struck –
courage will not fail us.
We are not afraid to face the bullets and die,
we are not bitter at being left homeless –
we will preserve you our Russian language,
the great Russian word.
Pure and free we will uphold you
and hand you on to our children's children,
and save you from captivity
forever!

[23 February 1942]

6–7 IN MEMORY OF A LENINGRAD BOY, MY NEIGHBOUR VALYA SMIRNOV

I

The lights are out.
Trenches are dug in the garden.
Petersburg's orphans
are my little children –
one can't breathe underground,
pain drills the forehead.
Through the bombing
a child's small voice is heard.

2

Knock with your little fist – I'll open up.
I always opened my door to you.
Now I've gone beyond the high mountain,
the desert, the wind and the blazing heat,
but I will never give you up . . .

I did not hear you crying
or asking me for bread.
Bring me a twig from the maple tree,
or just some blades of green grass
as you did last spring.
Bring me in your tiny cupped hands
some clear, cool water from our Neva,
and with my own hands I'll wipe clean
the blood from your little golden head.

[23 April 1942]
translated by Richard McKane

MIKLÓS RADNÓTI

The Seventh Eclogue

Can you see? As dark comes on, the barracks and the grim oak fence –
That is girded with barbed wire – dissolve: night soaks them up.
Slowly the eye relinquishes the bounds of our captivity
And the mind, only the mind, can tell how taut the wire is.
Do you see, dear? Even fancy has no other way to freedom;
The broken body's released by the fair deliverer, sleep;
And the prison camp, at such times, sets off for home.
In rags, their heads shaven, snoring, the prisoners fly
From the blind heights of Serbia to homelands now in hiding.
Homelands in hiding! Ah, does our home still exist?
It might have escaped the bombs? It still is – as when we left it?
Will that man who moans on my right, and this on my left, reach
          home?
Is there a land still, tell me, where this verse form has meaning?

Without putting in the accents, just groping line after line,
I write this poem here, in the dark, just as I live,
Half-blind, like a caterpillar inching my way across paper;
Torches, books – the *Lager* guards took everything;
And no post comes – just fog that settles upon the barracks.

Among false rumours and worms, we live here: with Frenchmen,
        Poles,
Heretic Serbs, loud Italians, nostalgic Jews, in the mountains.
This feverish body – dismembered, but still living one life – waits
For good news, for women's sweet words, for a life both free and
        human,
And the end plunged into obscurity, and miracles.

I lie on a plank, a captive beast among worms. Again
The fleas renew their assault, but the flies have gone to rest.
It's night, you see: captivity now is a day shorter.
And so is life. The camp is asleep. Over the land
The moon shines and the wires again go taut in its light;
Through the window you can see how the shadows of armed guards
Go pacing along on the wall through the noises of the night.

The camp is asleep. Do you see, my dear? Dreams fan their wings.
Someone starts, groans, turns in his tight space, and is
Already asleep again, his face aglow. Only I
Sit up awake – on my lips, instead of your kisses, the taste
Of a half-smoked cigarette; and no sleep comes bringing rest, for
I can no longer die without you, nor can I live.

Lager Heideman, in the mountains above Žagubica, July 1944
translated by Clive Wilmer and George Gömöri

MIKLÓS RADNÓTI

Forced March

A fool he is who, collapsed,   rises and walks again,
Ankles and knees moving   alone, like wandering pain,

Yet he, as if wings uplifted him,   sets out on his way,
And in vain the ditch calls him   back, who dare not stay.
And if asked why not, he might answer   – without leaving his path –
That his wife was awaiting him,   and a saner, more beautiful death.
Poor fool! He's out of his mind: now, for a long time,
Only scorched winds have whirled   over the houses at home,
The wall has been laid low,   the plum-tree is broken there,
The night of our native hearth   flutters, thick with fear.
O if only I could believe   that everything of worth
Were not just in my heart –   that I still had a home on earth;
If only I had! As before,   jam made fresh from the plum
Would cool on the old verandah,   in peace the bee would hum,
And an end-of-summer stillness   would bask in the drowsy garden,
Naked among the leaves   would sway the fruit-trees' burden,
And She would be waiting, blonde   against the russet hedgerow,
As the slow morning painted   slow shadow over shadow, –
Could it perhaps still be?   The moon tonight's so round!
Don't leave me friend, shout at me: I'll get up off the ground!

15 September 1944
translated by Clive Wilmer and George Gömöri

MIKLÓS RADNÓTI

Postcards

I

From Bulgaria, wild and swollen, the noise of cannon rolls;
It booms against the ridge, then hesitates, and falls.
Men, animals, carts, thoughts pile up as they fly;
The road rears back and whinnies, maned is the racing sky.
But you, in this shifting chaos, are what in me is constant:
In my soul's depth you shine forever – you are silent
And motionless, like an angel who marvels at destruction,
Or a beetle, burying, in a hollow tree's corruption.

In the mountains
30 August 1944

II

No more than nine kilometres away
Haystacks and houses flare;
There, on the meadows's verges, crouch the swains,
Pipe-smoking, dumb with fear.
Here still, where the tiny shepherdess steps in,
Ripples on the lake spread;
A flock of ruffled sheep bend over it
And drink the clouds they tread.

Cservenka
6 October 1944

III

Blood-red, the spittle drools from the oxen's mouths;
The men, stooping to urinate, pass blood;
The squad stands bunched in groups whose reek disgusts.
And loathsome Death blows overhead in gusts.

Mohács
24 October 1944

IV

I fell beside him. His body – which was taut
As a cord is, when it snaps – spun as It fell.
Shot in the neck. 'This is how you will end,'
I whispered to myself; 'keep lying still.
Now, patience is flowering into death.'
'*Der springt noch auf*,' said someone over me.
Blood on my ears was drying, caked with earth.

Szentkirályszabadja
31 October 1944

translated by Clive Wilmer and George Gömöri

JÁNOS PILINSKY

Frankfurt 1945

In the river bank, an empty sandpit –
all that summer we took the refuse there.
Gliding among villas and gardens
we came to a bridge. Then a dip of the road
and the wooden fence of the racetrack.
A few jolts, and the truck began to slow down.
But even before the brakes could tighten
the first surge of hunger overwhelmed us.

Among the spilling buckets and the bursting sacks –
horror of the spines, stooping into position!
Then among those toppled crates began
the pitiless pre-censorship,
interrogating the gristles of the offal.
And there, on all fours, hunger
could not stomach its own fury,
but revolted and surrendered.

They were lost in the dust and filth.
The whole truck shook, howling.
The swill clogged their hearts
and swamped their consciousness.
They burrowed to the bottoms of the filled cans
till their mouths and eyes were caked.
They drowned in that living sludge
and there they were resurrected with heads buried.

And they brought back, scrap by scrap,
what had been utterly lost with them,
wringing their salvation, drunkenly,
out of the gouged mush –
but before their joy could properly be seized
the poison of comprehension stirred.
First, only the bitterness in their mouths,
then their hearts tasted the full sadness.

Abruptly, they backed from the mob. Almost sober
they watched how this intoxication –
betraying their misery –
possessed their whole being.
But then again they abandoned themselves utterly,
now only enduring till their organs
cramming themselves, should have completed
the last mistake of gratification.

Only to get away – no matter where!
Only to get out, now!
The glowing pack drove us from them
without a flash! They did not even touch us.
All around – the blank walls of the pit.
Only to get home! Probably a steamer
went past quite close by on the river below
and its smoke and soot screened perfectly

the steep, crooked exit. Out across the field!
Bounding eagerly over the mounds
on to the flaming concrete. Then the villas!
The green world streaming back!
The wooden fence of the racecourse.
And after the volley of gaps between the palings
the torrid air, swooning from the gardens!
Then all at once – the shock of loneliness!

In a moment the splendour of the foliage burned out –
its flame hung darkly to the road.
And our faces, and our hands, darkened.
And with us, the paradise.
While behind us, between the jouncing cans
and the tattered dusty trees
emerged the crepuscular city
of Frankfurt – 1945.

translated by Ted Hughes and Janos Csokits

MITSUHARU KANEKO

Ascension

Today is execution day for the pacifists.
Escaping from the gunfire as their corpses topple,
Their souls have ascended to heaven.
To proclaim injustice and iniquity.

In grief, their spirits have begun to relent,
Calling from the edge
Of a great four-cornered ice-floe,
Turning to a rainbow flickering in the dark.

Bombs have exploded; fireworks have crackled:
Their souls, sent drifting to one corner of heaven,
Turned into mist, into spume, into cloud-drifts,
To stain the sky with blood that is still hot.

translated by Geoffrey Bownas and Anthony Thwaite

JÁNOS PILINSKY

Passion of Ravensbrück

He steps out from the others.
He stands in the square silence.
The prison garb, the convict's skull
blink like a projection.

He is horribly alone.
His pores are visible.
Everything about him is so gigantic,
everything is so tiny.

And this is all.
          The rest –
the rest was simply
that he forgot to cry out
before he collapsed.

translated by Ted Hughes and Janos Csokits

MIGUEL HERNANDEZ

Lullaby of the Onion

(Lines for his son, after receiving a letter from his wife in which
she said that all she had to eat was bread and onions.)

An onion is frost
shut in and poor.
Frost of your days
and of my nights.
Hunger and onion,
black ice and frost
huge and round.

My son is lying now
in the cradle of hunger.
The blood of an onion
is what he lives on.
But it is your blood,
with sugar on it like frost,
onion and hunger.

A dark woman
turned into moonlight
pours herself down thread
by thread over your cradle.
My son, laugh,
because you can swallow the moon
when you want to.

Lark of my house,
laugh often.
Your laugh is in your eyes
the light of the world.
Laugh so much
that my soul, hearing you
will beat wildly in space.

Your laugh unlocks doors for me,
it gives me wings.
It drives my solitudes off,
pulls away my jail.
Mouth that can fly,
heart that turns to
lightning on your lips.

Your laugh is the sword
that won all the wars,
it defeats the flowers
and the larks,
challenges the sun.
Future of my bones
and of my love.

The body with wings beating,
the eyelash so quick,
life is full of color
as it never was.
How many linnets
climb with wings beating
out of your body!

I woke up and was an adult:
don't wake up.
My mouth is sad:
you go on laughing.
In your cradle, forever,
defending your laughter
feather by feather.

Your being has a flying range
so high and so wide
that your body is a newly
born sky.
I wish I could climb
back to the starting point
of your travel!

You laugh, eight months old,
with five orange blossoms.
You have five tiny
ferocities.
You have five teeth
like five new
jasmine blossoms.

They will be the frontier
of kisses tomorrow,
when you feel your rows
of teeth are a weapon.
You will feel a flame
run along under your teeth
looking for the center.

My son, fly away, into the
two moons of the breast:
the breast, onion –
sad, but you, content.
Stay on your feet.
Stay ignorant of what's happening,
and what is going on.

translated by Robert Bly

BORIS SLUTSKY

How Did They Kill My Grandmother?

How did they kill my grandmother?
I'll tell you how they killed her.
One morning a tank rolled up to
a building where
the hundred and fifty Jews of our town who,
weightless
       from a year's starvation,
and white
       with the knowledge of death,
were gathered holding their bundles.

And the German polizei were
herding the old people briskly;
and their tin mugs clanked as
the young men led them away
                              far away.

But my small grandmother
my seventy-year old grandmother
began to curse and
scream at the Germans;
shouting that I was a soldier.
She yelled at them: My grandson
is off at the front fighting!
Don't you dare
touch me!
Listen, you
            can hear our guns!

Even as she went off, my grandmother
cried abuse,
            starting all over again
with her curses.
From every window then
Ivanovnas and Andreyevnas
Sidorovnas and Petrovnas
sobbed: You tell them, Polina
Matveyevna, keep it up!
They all yelled together:
            'What can we do against
this enemy, the Hun?'
Which was why the Germans chose
to kill her inside the town.

A bullet struck her hair
and kicked her grey plait down.
My grandmother fell to the ground.
That is how she died there.

translated by Elaine Feinstein

JOHANNES BOBROWSKI

Report

Bajla Gelblung,
escaped in Warsaw
from a transport from the Ghetto,
the girl took to the woods,
armed, was picked up
as partisan
in Brest-Litovsk,
wore a military coat (Polish),
was interrogated by German
officers, there is
a photo, the officers are young
chaps faultlessly uniformed,
with faultless faces,
their bearing
is unexceptionable.

translated by Ruth and Matthew Mead

CZESŁAW MIŁOSZ

A Poor Christian Looks at the Ghetto

Bees build around red liver,
Ants build around black bone.
It has begun: the tearing, the trampling on silks,
It has begun: the breaking of glass, wood, copper, nickel, silver, foam
Of gypsum, iron sheets, violin strings, trumpets, leaves, balls, crystals.
Poof! Phosphorescent fire from yellow walls
Engulfs animal and human hair.

Bees build around the honeycomb of lungs,
Ants build around white bone.
Torn is paper, rubber, linen, leather, flax,

[155]

Fibre, fabrics, cellulose, snakeskin, wire.
The roof and the wall collapse in flame and heat seizes the
foundations.
Now there is only the earth, sandy, trodden down,
With one leafless tree.

Slowly, boring a tunnel, a guardian mole makes his way,
With a small red lamp fastened to his forehead.
He touches burned bodies, counts them, pushes on,
He distinguishes human ashes by their luminous vapour,
The ashes of each man by a different part of the spectrum.
Bees build around a red trace.
Ants build around the place left by my body.

I am afraid, so afraid of the guardian mole.
He has swollen eyelids, like a Patriarch
Who has sat much in the light of candles
Reading the great book of the species.
What will I tell him, I, a Jew of the New Testament,
Waiting two thousand years for the second coming of Jesus?
My broken body will deliver me to his sight
And he will count me among the helpers of death:
The uncircumcised.

1943
translated by the poet

NOBUYUKI SAGA

The Myth of Hiroshima

What are they looking for,
running to the summit of lost time?
Hundreds of people vaporized instantly
are walking in mid-air.

'We didn't die.'
'We skipped over death in a flash and became spirits.'
'Give us a real, human death.'

One man's shadow among hundreds is branded on stone steps.

'Why am I imprisoned in stone?'
'Where did my flesh go, separated from its shadow?'
'What must I wait for?'

The twentieth century myth is stamped with fire.
Who will free this shadow from the stone?

translated by Hajime Kajima

TAMIKI HARA

Glittering Fragments

Glittering fragments
Ashen embers
Like a rippling panorama,
Burning red then dulled.
Strange rhythm of human corpses.
All existence, all that could exist
Laid bare in a flash. The rest of the world
The swelling of a horse's corpse
At the side of an upturned train,
The smell of smouldering electric wires.

translated by Geoffrey Bownas and Anthony Thwaite

SANKICHI TOGE

At a First Aid Post

You
Who have no channels for tears when you weep
No lips through which words can issue when you howl
No skin for your fingers to grip with when you writhe in torment
You

Your squirming limbs all smeared with blood and slimy sweat and
    lymph
Between your closed lids the glaring eyeballs show only a thread of
    white
On your pale swollen bellies only the perished elastic that held up
    your drawers
You who now can no longer feel shame at exposing your sheltered
    sex
O who could believe that
Only minutes ago
You were all schoolgirls fresh and appealing

In scorched and raw Hiroshima
Out of dark shuddering flames
You no longer the human creatures you had been
Scrambled and crawled one after the other
Dragged yourselves along as far as this open ground
To bury in the dusts of agony
Your frizzled hair on skulls almost bare as heads of Buddhist saints

Why should you have to suffer like this
Why suffer like this
What is the reason
What reason
And you
Do not know
How you look nor
What your humanity has been turned into

You are remembering
Simply remembering
Those who until this morning were
Your fathers mothers brothers sisters
(Would any of them recognize you now if they met you)
Remembering your homes where you used to sleep wake eat
(In a single flash all the flowers on their hedges were blasted
And no one knows where their ashes lie)
Remembering remembering
Here with your fellow-creatures who one by one gradually moving
Remembering

Those days when
You were daughters
Daughters of humankind.

translated by James Kirkup

TAMIKI HARA

this is a Human Being

this is a human being
look what an A-bomb has done to it
the flesh swells so horribly
and both men and women are reduced to one form
'Help me!' says the faint cry
leaking from the swelled lips, the terribly
burned mess of a festered face
this, this is a human being
this is a man's face

translated by Geoffrey Bownas and Anthony Thwaite

VI

'Speechless, you testify against us'

DAN PAGIS

Scrawled in Pencil in a Sealed Railway Car

> here in this transport
> i eve
> and abel my son
> if you should see my older son
> cain son of man
> tell him that i

translated by Stephen Mitchell

PAUL CELAN

Death Fugue

Black milk of dawn we drink it at dusk
we drink it at noon and at daybreak we drink it at night
we drink it and drink it
we are digging a grave in the air there's room for us all
A man lives in the house he plays with the serpents he writes
he writes when it darkens to Germany your golden hair Margarete
he writes it and steps outside and the stars all aglisten he whistles for
        his hounds
he whistles for his Jews he has them dig a grave in the earth
he commands us to play for the dance

Black milk of dawn we drink you at night
we drink you at daybreak and noon we drink you at dusk
we drink and we drink
A man lives in the house he plays with the serpents he writes
he writes when it darkens to Germany your golden hair Margarete
Your ashen hair Shulamite we are digging a grave in the air there's
        room for us all

He shouts cut deeper in the earth to some the rest of you sing and
        play

he reaches for the iron in his belt he heaves it his eyes are blue
make your spades cut deeper the rest of you play for the dance

Black milk of dawn we drink you at night
we drink you at noon and at daybreak we drink you at dusk
we drink and we drink
a man lives in the house your golden hair Margarete
your ashen hair Shulamite he plays with the serpents

He shouts play death more sweetly death is a master from Germany
he shouts play the violins darker you'll rise as smoke in the air
then you'll have a grave in the clouds there's room for you all

translated by Michael Hamburger

POEMS BY TWO CHILDREN FROM TEREZIN
Homesick

I've lived in the ghetto here more than a year,
In Terezin, in the black town now,
And when I remember my old home so dear,
I can love it more than I did, somehow.

Ah, home, home,
Why did they tear me away?
Here the weak die easy as a feather
And when they die, they die forever.

I'd like to go back home again,
It makes me think of sweet spring flowers.
Before, when I used to live at home,
It never seemed so dear and fair.

I remember now those golden days . . .
But maybe I'll be going there soon again.

People walk along the street,
You see at once on each you meet
That there's a ghetto here,
A place of evil and of fear.

There's little to eat and much to want,
Where bit by bit, it's horror to live.
But no one must give up!
The world turns and times change.

Yet we all hope the time will come
When we'll go home again.
Now I know how dear it is
And often I remember it.

Anonymous
1943

Terezin

The heaviest wheel rolls across our foreheads
To bury itself deep somewhere inside our memories.

We've suffered here more than enough,
Here in this clot of grief and shame,
Wanting a badge of blindness
To be a proof for their own children.

A fourth year of waiting, like standing above a swamp
From which any moment might gush forth a spring.

Meanwhile, the rivers flow another way,
Another way,
Not letting you die, not letting you live.

And the cannons don't scream and the guns don't bark
And you don't see blood here.

Nothing, only silent hunger.
Children steal the bread here and ask and ask
    and ask
And all would wish to sleep, keep silent and
    just to go to sleep again. . . .

The heaviest wheel rolls across our foreheads
To bury itself deep somewhere inside our memories.

Mif
1944

NELLY SACHS

Even The Old Men's Last Breath

Even the old men's last breath
That had already grazed death
You snatched away.
The empty air
Trembling
To fill the sigh of relief
That thrusts this earth away –
You have plundered the empty air!

The old men's
Parched eyes
You pressed once more
Till you reaped the salt of despair –
All that this star owns
Of the contortions of agony,
All suffering from the dungeons of worms
Gathered in heaps –

O you thieves of genuine hours of death,
Last breaths and the eyelids' Good Night
Of one thing be sure:

The angel, it gathers
What you discarded,
From the old men's premature midnight
A wind of last breaths shall arise
And drive this unloosed star
Into its Lord's hands!

translated by Michael Hamburger

NELLY SACHS

A Dead Child Speaks

My mother held me by my hand.
Then someone raised the knife of parting:
So that it should not strike me,
My mother loosed her hand from mine.
But she lightly touched my thighs once more
And her hand was bleeding –

After that the knife of parting
Cut in two each bite I swallowed –
It rose before me with the sun at dawn
And began to sharpen itself in my eyes –
Wind and water ground in my ear
And every voice of comfort pierced my heart –

As I was led to death
I still felt in the last moment
The unsheathing of the great knife of parting.

translated by Michael Hamburger

ANNA KAMIEŃSKA

Names

'Not to ignore a single sacrifice and not to forget a single grave'
(SZYMON DATNER, 55 Days of the Wehrmacht in Poland)

They come dressed in their graves
sleeves too tight
How many years they have come
Is it eternity yet they ask
is there another to come
Eternity cannot be nameless
Names are there to exist in

to arise from the pulp of the murdered
to lean on the elbow of a name
Let mother call for me
let a woman name me in love's embrace

Ascend the stairs of names
upwards upwards
there are storeys of dead human clay
ascend the stairs of surnames
of open mouth half-closed lids

Beautiful words long ago
turned their backs like doors
and one still reads in that school
the list of absentees

Aronson Izaak
Brzostowski Szymon
Gąska Jan
Gelibter Rachmiel
Kwiatkowski Fraciszek
Poboży Antoni
Zając Wacław

No need to compose poems
let us chant names
let us pray to our God
with lists of the murdered

translated by Tomasz P. Krzeszowski and Desmond Graham

STANISLAW WYGODSKI

Those Betrayed at Dawn

Those betrayed at dawn,
were already dead by noon,
the men betrayed at noon,
were already dead by night.
Those awaiting betrayal, alert
till dawn,

till noon,
till night,
were killed year by year.

translated by Isaac Komem

FIVE POEMS BY LUBA KRUGMAN GURDUS

Birthday

Joy and laughter
What a lovely day
Bobus turned three
Let's celebrate

Yet another year
We have all survived
To celebrate his birthday
And laud the clement skies

This was years ago –
All that's left is pain
On my mournful lips
Hangs a mute complaint . . .

Nobody Knows My Pain

Nobody knows my pain,
Save these pages filled
With words slowly draining
From my wounds . . .
Save the sky,
Which welcomes my teary gaze
And linens,
Soothing my swollen lids

Nobody knows my pain,
Save the golden sun,
Which invades with rays

My closely veiled eyes
Save the wind,
Which strokes my moistened lash
And the cloud,
Suspended high above

Roll-Call

Darkness recedes after the short night
Revealing corpses in shallow mud
Many still breathing, barely alive
Wasted by sickness, frozen, starved . . .

Rows and rows of women, in black-gray rags
Wait in front of barracks for the morning count
Their feet covered by snow and slush
And bodies torpid in bitter cold

Long hours pass before the tedious check
By the Nazi mistress with her torture gear
And the hateful Capo, always at her side
Their faces marked by an odious sneer

The roll-call of the living and the dead ends
In count of those gone and those still abused
By hunger, thirst and hard slave work
Before ending in ovens or on gallow hooks

Majdanek

All lost its shape in the dense fog
Save the dimly lit, snowy track
Lined with armed towers, looming high
And search lights, neatly spaced apart

Of the twelve fields we quickly passed
Only one betrayed a feverish rush
With inmates pushing heavy carts
Loaded with corpses, probably gassed

Our truck stopped at gate thirteen
With sentry boxes at opposite ends
Guarding a huge field of unblemished white
Surrounded by a high voltage fence

Along the field small houses in rows
Like entrenched medieval forts
With narrow windows, adorned by frost
And snow-sprinkled wide opened doors

Inside the empty barracks, offensive smells
Mixed with a strong carbolic scent
Attacking nostrils, eyes and throats
With dense and heavy fetoric stench

The barracks seemed emptied in stride
On its three-levelled wooden bunks
Remnants of inmates' gloves and shawls
Traces of violence and fight

Inside the barracks bitter cold
Outside, Majdanek in its glory,
Covered by blankets of snowy white
Under a sapphire, star-studded sky

Last Supper

Soup simmers quietly
And it's hard to bear
That this is the last supper
We will ever share

We sit all together
Letting Mother serve
Her nourishing peasoup
So lovingly prepared

The rattling of wood spoons
Irritates my ears
But calms my aching heart
Soothing mounting fears

Our bundles are ready,
Pots, pans, underwear
Bobus has also added
His tiny teddy bear

Early in the morning
We'll surely be moved
To the Collection Center
With the local Jews

Then we will be pushed
To waiting cattle cars
And wild Nazi shouts
Will stifle babies' cries

The windows will be barred
The doors closed tight
We'll be pushed and abused
Against all human right

I finished my peasoup
And covered the moist eyes
This is our last supper
And our last goodbye . . .

translated by the poet

CHARLES REZNIKOFF

from *Holocaust*

In the gas chambers
the police wedged the people closely together
until men and women were standing on the feet of each other
and the doors were closed.
But the engine to furnish the gas
could not start.
An hour or two and almost three went by,
and in the gas chamber cries were heard
and many were praying.

The Professor who had been holding his ear against one of the wooden
        doors
turned away, smiled and said, 'Just like a synagogue.'
And then the engine started working:
in about half an hour all inside the gas chambers were dead.

When the rear doors were opened,
those inside were standing like statues:
there had been no room to fall
or even bend.
Among the dead, families were to be seen,
holding each other by the hand,
hands tightly clasped
so that those who threw out the dead
had trouble parting them.

The bodies were thrown out quickly
for other transports were coming:
bodies blue, wet with sweat and urine, legs covered in excrement,
and everywhere the bodies of babies and children.
Two dozen workers were busy
opening the mouths of the dead with iron hooks
and with chisels taking out teeth with golden caps;
and elsewhere other workers were tearing open the dead
looking for money or jewels that might have been swallowed.
And all the bodies were thrown into the large pits dug near the gas
        chambers
to be covered with sand.

ABRAHAM SUTZKEVER

To My Child

Out of hunger
or out of great love –
but your mother can witness to it –
I wanted to swallow you, my child,
when I felt your small body cool

[173]

in my fingers,
as if I pressed in them
a warm glass of tea
and felt it turning cold.

Since you are no stranger, no guest,
on our earth one does not birth another:
one births oneself like a ring
and the rings link in chains together.

My child,
who in words is called: love,
and who without words are yourself love,
you – the seed of my every dream,
the hidden third,
who from the wides of the world
with the wonder of an unseen storm
have made two meet and flow together
to create you and complete our pleasure:-

Why did you darken the creation
as you did when you shut your eyes
and left me outside like a beggar
with a world blanketed in snow
which you shook off?

No cradle, whose every motion
holds within the rhythm of the stars,
had brought you joy.
The sun – for you have never seen it shine –
might as well crack and shatter like glass.
A drop of poison burned out your faith.
You thought
it was warm sweet milk.

I wanted to swallow you, my child,
to know the taste
of my anticipated future.
Perhaps you will blossom as before
in my veins.

But I am not worthy to be your grave.
So I bequeath you
to the summoning snow,
the snow – my first respite –
and you will sink
like a splinter of dusk
into the quiet depths
and bear greetings from me
to the small shoots beneath the cold.

Vilna Ghetto, 18 January 1943
translated by David G. Roskies and Hillel Schwartz

ZBIGNIEW HERBERT

Warsaw Cemetery

This wall
of the last view
is not here

lime for houses and graves
lime for memory

the last echo of a salvo
formed into a stone slab
and a terse inscription
engraved in peaceful Roman script

the dead flee the invasion of the living
they descend more deeply
lower down

they complain at night in the pipes of sorrow
they come out cautiously
drop by drop

once again they flare up
with the simple scratch of a match

and on the surface calm
slabs lime for memory

on the corner of an avenue of the living
and the new world
under the proudly knocking heel
gathers like a molehill
the cemetery of those who ask
for a mound of loose earth
for a faint sign from above the surface

translated by John Carpenter and Bogdana Carpenter

MIROSLAV HOLUB

Sunday

The Marathon runners have reached the turning point:
Sunday, that day of sad songs
by the railway bridge
and the clouds.
                    Your eyes, at zenith –
and to say this without using the body is
like running without touching the ground.

            Thirty years ago
a transport passed here, open wagons
loaded with silhouettes,
with heads and shoulders cut out
from the black paper of horror.
And these people loved somebody,
but the train returns empty
every Sunday, only
a few hairgrips
and cinders
on the wagon floor.

Who know how to touch the ground,
who knows how not to touch the ground?

No choice but to believe
in the existence of the Marathon's finishing line
in two hours and forty minutes,
amidst the deafening din of the clouds
and of empty open wagons
on the railway bridge.

translated by Ian and Jarmila Milner

ANNA KAMIEŃSKA
Dr Korczak's Lie

You must admit you have lied to your children doctor
you have lied to two hundred of your children
and then you decided to lie to them to the end
which means to the very ramp and even further
and if it had been possible into the ear of death itself
you would have whispered to them the benediction of your lie

It is true you could not have done otherwise
because the truth became deadly
while the world made from the word light became
prohibited for children
like too true a film
In fact the world itself turned by so many degrees
so that truth became lie
and lie which should have been truth
found shelter in your Jewish orphanage

Perhaps they guessed something foresaw
at times you caught their anxious looks
perhaps Moniuś perhaps Abrasza the quick one
little Mendel wept in his sleep
their faces carried a gleam like old men's faces
haven't you long learnt from children how to die

Look doctor
this is your writing
The Holy Book of Children

they come out of a new Bible
little Romcia Rachel and Ruth
Davidek Zigmuś Aron and Jacubek
from that Book from that biblical land
from that lie which used to be truth
always on the road
with a bundle
with a starvation knapsack
from that dough
from that body
from that ancient blood
from that love
from that toil
from those burnt graphs of weight and height
from that suffering
from that vigil
from that death

And here how silent here after their weeping
after their screaming
how silent this slaughterhouse of children
this land this land
doctor

translated by Tomasz P. Krzesowski and Desmond Graham

TADEUSZ RÓŻEWICZ
Pigtail

When all the women in the transport
had their heads shaved
four workmen with brooms made of birch twigs
swept up
and gathered up the hair

Behind clean glass
the stiff hair lies
of those suffocated in gas chambers
there are pins and side combs
in this hair

The hair is not shot through with light
is not parted by the breeze
is not touched by any hand
or rain or lips

In huge chests
clouds of dry hair
of those suffocated
and a faded plait
a pigtail with a ribbon
pulled at school
by naughty boys.

The Museum, Auschwitz, 1948
translated by Adam Czerniawski

TADEUSZ RÓŻEWICZ

Massacre of the Boys

The children cried 'Mummy!
But I have been good!
It's dark in here! Dark!'

See them They are going to the bottom
See the small feet
they went to the bottom Do you see
that print
of a small foot here and there

pockets bulging
with string and stones
and little horses made of wire

A great plain closed
like a figure of geometry
and a tree of black smoke
a vertical
dead tree
with no star in its crown

The Museum, Auschwitz, 1948
translated by Adam Czerniawski

ÁGNES GERGELY

Crazed Man in Concentration Camp

All through the march, besides bag and blanket
he carried in his hands two packages of empty boxes,
and when the company halted for a couple of minutes
he laid the two packages of empty boxes neatly at each side,
being careful not to damage or break either of them,
the parcels were of
ornamental boxes
dovetailed by sizes each to each
and tied together with packing-cord,
the top box with a picture on it.
When the truck was about to start, the sergeant
shouted something in sergeant's language,
they sprang up suddenly,
and one of the boxes rolled down to the wheel,
the smallest one, the one with the picture:
'It's fallen,' he said and made to go after it,
but the truck moved off
and his companions held his hands
while his hands held the two packages of boxes
and his tears trailed down his jacket.
'It's fallen,' he said that evening in the queue—
and it meant nothing to him to be shot dead.

translated by Edwin Morgan

DAN PAGIS

Instructions for Crossing the Border

Imaginary man, go. Here is your passport.
You are not allowed to remember.
You have to match the description:
your eyes are already blue.
Don't escape with the sparks
inside the smokestack:

you are a man, you sit in the train.
Sit comfortably.
You've got a decent coat now,
a repaired body, a new name
ready in your throat.
Go, You are not allowed to forget.

translated by Stephen Mitchell

ABRAHAM SUTZKEVER

How?

How will you fill your goblet
On the day of liberation? And with what?
Are you prepared, in your joy, to endure
The dark keening you have heard
Where skulls of days glitter
In a bottomless pit?

You will search for a key to fit
Your jammed locks. You will bite
The sidewalks like bread,
Thinking: It used to be better.
And time will gnaw at you like a cricket
Caught in a fist.

Then your memory will resemble
An ancient buried town.
And your estranged eyes will burrow down
Like a mole, a mole. . . .

Vilna Ghetto, 14 February 1943
translated by Chana Bloch

ABRAHAM SUTZKEVER

from *Epitaphs*

This man could be a god, and I a worm.
All the same I roar at my tormentor:
  You have no right.

That I die, in witness, arm across my chest,
  Is nothing.
But that a slave should be master of my years—
  This, to me, is gall.

• • •

Inscribed on the slat of a railway car:

Should you happen on a string of pearls,
Threaded on a length of blood-red silk,
Which, like the pathway of life, runs all the finer
As it nears the throat,
Until, dissolved in fog,
It vanishes from sight—

Know, these pearls you've found
Once coolly lit my heart,
The reckless eighteen-year-old heart
Of a Paris showgirl named Marie.

I, transported through chartless Poland,
Now fling them through the grate.

If you are a man,
Deck your sweetheart with your find.
Wear them, if a girl,
The pearls are yours.
And if old – let them form
The object of your prayers.

Hangman, beware. Your every savagery
Is aimed against you, tenfold.
Even here, in this oven hell,
My burning soul is not consumed.

Curling from chimneys, a cloud of black,
I will come swarming, gliding on your trail,
Obliterating trace and spore,
Your serpent in his cradle, your domain.

In an orchard, amid the fruit trees,
On the drawbeam of a well,
A scratching:
Here lie those not present
When village folk were in the synagogue,
Being burned.

With the well-rope,
He who blindly writes these words
Has hoisted from this grave of waters
Himself and child.
Now he but desires
To return below.

Vilna Ghetto – Moscow – Lodz 1943–6
translated by Neal Kozodoy

JÁNOS PILINSKY

On the Wall of a KZ-Lager

Where you have fallen, you stay.
In the whole universe, this is your place.
Just this single spot.
But you have made this yours absolutely.

The countryside evades you.
House, mill, poplar,
each thing strives to be free of you
as if it were mutating in nothingness.

But now it is you who stay.
Did we blind you? You continue to watch us.
Did we rob you? You enriched yourself.
Speechless, speechless, you testify against us.

translated by Ted Hughes and Janos Csokits

PRIMO LEVI

Buna

Torn feet and cursed earth,
The long line in the grey morning.
The Buna smokes from a thousand chimneys,
A day like every other day awaits us.
The whistles terrible at dawn:
'You multitudes with dead faces,
On the monotonous horror of the mud
Another day of suffering is born.'
Tired companion, I see you in my heart.
I read your eyes, sad friend.
In your breast you carry cold, hunger, nothing.
You have broken what's left of the courage within you.
Colourless one, you were a strong man,
A woman walked at your side.
Empty companion who no longer has a name,
Forsaken man who can no longer weep,
So poor you no longer grieve,
So tired you no longer fear.
Spent once-strong man.
If we were to meet again
Up there in the world, sweet beneath the sun,
With what kind of face would we confront each other?

28 December 1945
translated by Ruth Feldman and Brian Swann

[184]

PRIMO LEVI

Singing

. . . But when we started singing
Those good foolish songs of ours,
Then everything was again
As it always had been.

A day was just a day,
And seven make a week.
Killing seemed an evil thing to us;
Dying – something remote.

The months pass rather quickly,
But there are still so many left!
Once more we were just young men:
Not martyrs, not infamous, not saints.

This and other things came into our minds
While we kept singing.
But they were cloudlike things,
Hard to explain.

3 January 1946
translated by Ruth Feldman and Brian Swann

PRIMO LEVI

25 February 1944

I would like to believe in something,
Something beyond the death that undid you.
I would like to describe the intensity
With which, already overwhelmed,
We longed in those days to be able
To walk together once again
Free beneath the sun.

9 January 1946
translated by Ruth Feldman and Brian Swann

PRIMO LEVI
Shemà

You who live secure
In your warm houses,
Who return at evening to find
Hot food and friendly faces:

    Consider whether this is a man,
    Who labours in the mud
    Who knows no peace
    Who fights for a crust of bread
    Who dies at a yes or a no.
    Consider whether this is a woman,
    Without hair or name
    With no more strength to remember
    Eyes empty and womb cold
    As a frog in winter.

Consider that this has been:
I commend these words to you.
Engrave them on your hearts
When you are in your house, when you walk on your way,
When you go to bed, when you rise.
Repeat them to your children.
Or may your house crumble,
Disease render you powerless,
Your offspring avert their faces from you.

10 January 1946
translated by Ruth Feldman and Brian Swann

VII

'I am twenty-four led to slaughter
I survived'

TADEUSZ RÓŻEWICZ

The Survivor

I am twenty-four
led to slaughter
I survived.

The following are empty synonyms:
man and beast
love and hate
friend and foe
darkness and light.

The ways of killing men and beasts are the same
I've seen them:
truckfuls of chopped-up men
who will not be saved.

Ideas are mere words:
virtue and crime
truth and lies
beauty and ugliness
courage and cowardice.

Virtue and crime weigh the same
I've seen it:
in a man who was both
criminal and virtuous.

I seek a teacher and a master
may he restore my sight hearing and speech
may he once more name ideas and objects
may he separate darkness from light.

I am twenty-four
led to slaughter
I survived.

translated by Adam Czerniawski

MARC KAMINSKY

from *To Give Comfort*

Days
of torrential rain
relieve us
of the August sun

weeds
and wild flowers
bloom
riotously

at their first
taste of
sweet potato
since the bombing

patients
throughout the ward
murmur
'*Oishii!*'

and I
startle everyone – and myself—
    crying
violently and without shame

for my daughters

CHAIM GRADE

The Miracle

Because everything I build is built on the miracle
that I survive, panic storms me.
When you go away for an hour out of twenty-four,
don't let the emptiness betray too suddenly
that you're only here in my imagination;
because everything I build is built on a marvel,
and when you go away for an hour, that hour becomes
a long drawnout struckdumb century.
I see that my house is made of fog and smoke,
that the water again has overflowed its banks,
and you're only a dream, an invention of mine
that will fade away in separate moments.

Sometimes I cross a street and I ask:
Did I just walk over a covered grave?
For since I've seen marvels on my way,
I see a world of hidden graves.
Sometimes I stand before my house, forgetting
that this is my house, and my heart howls out;
because everything I build is built on a miracle,
and may become topsy turvy in the flick of an eyelash.
The miracle makes me sick, old-grey and tired,
and only in my memory am I any younger.
Thus I live like a war invalid
with sensations of shot-off fingers.

translated by Ruth Whitman

MARC KAMINSKY

Carrying My Brother

THE SHOPKEEPER'S ASSISTANT

I am still on the road to the doctor's house
carrying my brother
in my arms
thinking: he is going to survive

He was five months old
and all I could give him was gruel—
thin gruel
there were no spots on his body

A week after the bomb fell
he began to look better
I was pleased—
he was the only one I had left

and while we were on the road
to the doctor's house
he died
I found two big spots on his bottom

And I have never been able to escape
my loneliness and fear
even now
I find myself going to the mirror

three and four times a day, dropping
my pants, and looking for purple spots
and always nervously touching
my hair, and checking my gums

never sure
where some sign of the disease
will show itself
I am always on the road to the doctor

KÔICHI IIJIMA

The End of the War to End All Wars

1 A SKY FOR STRANGERS

The birds came down.
They pecked in cracks made in the earth.
Flew hovering
above the unfamiliar roofs.
They seemed uncertain, bewildered.

The sky holds its head
as though it had eaten stone,
plunged now in grief.
The bloodshed's stopped
but all the blood's still circling in the sky
like strangers wondering at the calm.

2 OUT OF THE SAND

Bean-stalks are growing out of the sand,
potatoes too.
He searched.
For the friendly face
that had fallen into the earth.
And then for his own lost face.

Years I lived through
stained with evil
went whipping past my ear.
The calendars shredded, fluttering.

Years when people like wild dogs
in the dug-outs awkwardly
squatted down and wept.

translated by Harry and Lynn Guest and Kajimo Shozo

MARC KAMINSKY

Every Month

THE TEN-YEAR-OLD GIRL

My house
was close to the place where the bomb fell

My mother
was turned to white bone before
the family altar

Grandfather and I
go to visit her on the sixth of every month

Mother
is now living in the temple at Nakajima

Mother
must be so pleased
to see how big I've gotten

but all I see
is the Memorial Panel quietly standing there
no matter how I try
I can't remember what Mother looks like

GÜNTER EICH

Inventory

This is my cap,
this is my coat,
here's my shaving gear
in a linen sack.

A can of rations:
my plate, my cup,
I've scratched my name
in the tin.

Scratched it with this
valuable nail
which I hide
from avid eyes.

In the foodsack is
a pair of wool socks
and something else that I
show to no one,

it all serves as a pillow
for my head at night.
The cardboard here lies
between me and the earth.

The lead in my pencil
I love most of all:
in the daytime it writes down
the verses I make at night.

This is my notebook,
this is my tarpaulin,
this is my towel,
this is my thread.

translated by Stuart Friebert

RACHEL KORN

Lot's Wife

I wasn't brave enough to turn
when my home was burned
and my happiness was torn away.
I envy you
for turning in mid-flight
turning to salty stone
to guard the love you felt.

Fearing exile more than God's anger,
your longing was stronger than his hard punishing word.
Your home nested in your eyes,
cradle, orchard, flocks of sheep,
in that split-second when eternity conquered.

Now you watch over all your dreams,
and the bare mountains and the dead sea.
The blood trickles into your limbs at sunset;
reflecting the flame,
your body shimmers in the pink light, young again,
and you smile, remembering,
a smile of betrothal to your own name—
you are yourself again, no longer just your husband's wife.

I wasn't brave enough to turn,
and my heart turned to a clod of stone,
and the word turns to salt on my lips,
the taste of my unfinished tears.

translated by Seymour Levitan

DAN PAGIS

The Roll Call

He stands, stamps a little in his boots,
rubs his hands. He's cold in the morning breeze:
a diligent angel, who has worked hard for his promotions.
Suddenly he thinks he's made a mistake: all eyes,
he counts again in the open notebook
all the bodies waiting for him in the square,
camp within camp: only I
am not there, am not there, am a mistake,
turn off my eyes, quickly, erase my shadow.
I shall not want. The sum will be in order
without me: here for eternity.

translated by Stephen Mitchell

RACHEL KORN

My Mother Often Wept

A birch tree may be growing on the mound
heaped by a murderer's hands
in thick woods near the town of Greyding,
and only a bird goes there to honour the dead

where my mother lies in an unknown grave,
a German bullet in her heart.
And I go, go, go there only in dreams,
my eyes shut, my mouth dumb.

I remember that my mother often wept,
and I, I imagined
Abraham's son, bound for the sacrifice, looking to her
from the pages of her prayerbook
while she lived Sarah's fate

and we tumbled, laughed, and played,
despite our father's early death—
Had he lived, our good father,
he would never, never
have taken us to Mount Moriah to be sacrificed.

And yet my mother wept so often—
Did she know
that heaven had prepared
to open wide its gates
and take her sons
in billowing clouds of smoke?

And I was left behind, her only daughter,
like a thorn in dry ground,
and I am the voice of my mother's tears,
I am the sound
of her weeping.

translated by Seymour Levitan

SÁNDOR WEÖRES

Whisper in the Dark

From a well you mount up, dear child. Your head a pyre, your arm a stream, your trunk air, your feet mud. I shall bind you, but don't be afraid: I love you and my bonds are your freedom.

On your head I write: 'I am strong, devoted, secure, and home-loving, like one who wants to please women.'

On your arm I write: 'I have plenty of time, I am in no hurry: I have eternity.'

On your trunk I write: 'I am poured into everything and everything pours into me: I am not fastidious, but who is there who could defile me?'

On your feet I write: 'I have measured the darkness and my hand troubles its depths; nothing could sink so deep that I should not be deeper.'

You have turned to gold, dear child. Change yourself into bread for the blind and swords for those who can see.

1946
translated by Edwin Morgan

TADEUSZ RÓŻEWICZ

In the Midst of Life

After the end of the world
after death
I found myself in the midst of life
creating myself
building life
people animals landscapes

this is a table I said
this is a table
there is bread and a knife on the table

knife serves to cut bread
people are nourished by bread

man must be loved
I learnt by night by day
what must one love
I would reply man

this is a window I said
this is a window
there is a garden beyond the window
I see an apple-tree in the garden
the apple-tree blossoms
the blossom falls
fruit is formed
ripens

my father picks the apple
the man who picks the apple
is my father

I sat on the threshold

that old woman who
leads a goat on a string
is needed more
is worth more
than the seven wonders of the world
anyone who thinks or feels
she is not needed
is a mass murderer

this is a man
this is a tree this is bread

people eat to live
I kept saying to myself
human life is important
human life has great importance

the value of life
is greater than the value of all things
which man has created
man is a great treasure
I repeated stubbornly

this is water I said
I stroked the waves with my hand
and talked to the river
water I would say
nice water
this is me

man talked to water
talked to the moon
to the flowers and to rain

talked to the earth
to the birds
to the sky

the sky was silent
the earth was silent
and if a voice was heard
flowing
from earth water and sky
it was a voice of another man

1955
translated by Adam Czerniawski

JÁNOS PILINSKY
The French Prisoner

If only I could forget that Frenchman.
I saw him, just before dawn, creeping past our quarters
into the dense growth of the back garden
so that he almost merged into the ground.

As I watched he looked back, he peered all round –
at last he had found a safe hideout.
Now his plunder can be all his!
He'll go no further, whatever happens.

Already he is eating, biting into the turnip
which he must have smuggled out under his rags.
He was gulping raw cattle-turnip!
Yet he had hardly swallowed one mouthful
before it flooded back up.
Then the sweet pulp in his mouth mingled
with delight and disgust the same
as the unhappy and happy come together
in their bodies' voracious ecstasy.

Only to forget that body, those quaking shoulder blades,
the hands shrunk to bone,
the bare palm that crammed at his mouth, and clung there
so that it ate, too.
And the shame, desperate and enraged
of the organs embittered against each other
forced to tear from each other
their last bonds of kinship.

The way his clumsy feet had been left out
of the gibbering bestial joy
and splayed there, crushed beneath
the rapture and torture of his body.
And his glance – if only I could forget that!
Though he was choking, he kept on
forcing more down his gullet – no matter what –
only to eat – anything – this – that – even himself!

Why go on. Guards came for him.
He had escaped from the nearby prison camp.
And just as I did then, in that garden,
I am strolling here, among garden shadows, at home.
I look into my notes and quote:
'If only I could forget that Frenchman . . .'
And from my ears, my eyes, my mouth
the scalding memory shouts at me:

'I am hungry!' And suddenly I feel
the eternal hunger
which that poor creature has long ago forgotten
and which no earthly nourishment can lessen.
He lives on me. And more and more hungrily!
And I am less and less sufficient for him.
And now he, who would have eaten anything,
is clamouring for my heart.

translated by Ted Hughes and Janos Csokits

ABBA KOVNER

Observation at Dawn

The night is still silky. Curtains are drawn
from the edge of the dream in a slow rhythm.
Red silk. We are both awake
trying quietly to spin the thread
cut off between the ribs. I'm reluctant
to look at this rain
beating at the windows.

And inside, the night
is still silky. Your breath a soft thicket
guarding its border. When I count
the number of pulse beats, as if not believing,
and find signs in them, suddenly my eyes
discover my body (my arms stretched out) lying here
naked (must I retrieve them somehow?).

Rain
it's just rain! Like an oath I repeat
for the third time. Not your blood.
Then my finger taps on your throat
groping like a blind man's cane.

translated by Shirley Kaufmann

RACHEL KORN

Sometimes I Want to Go Up

Sometimes I want to go up
on tiptoe
to a strange house
and feel the walls with my hands –
what kind of clay is baked in the bricks,
what kind of wood is in the door,
and what kind of god has pitched his tent here,
to guard it from misfortune and ruin?

What kind of swallow under the roof
has built its nest from straw and earth
and what kind of angels disguised as men
came here as guests?

What holy men came out to meet them,
bringing them basins of water
to wash the dust from their feet,
the dust of earthly roads?

And what blessing did they leave
the children – from big to small,
that it could protect and guard them
from Belzec, Maidanek, Treblinka?

From just such a house,
fenced in with a painted railing,
in the middle of trees and blooming flowerbeds,
blue, gold, flame,
there came out –
the murderer of my people,
of my mother.

I'll let my sorrow grow
like Samson's hair long ago,
and I'll turn the millstone of days
around this bloody track.

Until one night
when I hear over me
the murderer's drunken laugh,
I'll tear the door from its hinges
and I'll rock the building –
till the night wakes up
from the shaking coming through every pane,
every brick, every nail, every board of the house,
from the very ground to the roof –

Although I know, I know, my God,
that the falling walls
will bury only me
and my sorrow.

translated by Ruth Whitman

TADEUSZ RÓŻEWICZ

The Dead Have Remembered

The dead have remembered
our indifference
The dead have remembered
our silence
The dead have remembered
our words

The dead see our snouts
laughing from ear to ear
The dead see
our bodies rubbing against each other
The dead see our hands
poised for applause

The dead read our books
listen to our speeches
delivered so long ago

the dead hear
clucking tongues

The dead scrutinize our lectures
join in previously terminated
discussions

The dead see stadiums
ensembles and choirs declaiming rhythmically

All the living are guilty

little children
who offered bouquets of flowers
are guilty
lovers are guilty
guilty are

guilty are those who ran away
and those that stayed
those who were saying yes
those who said no
and those who said nothing

the dead are taking stock of the living
the dead will not rehabilitate us

1957
translated by Adam Czerniawski

AMIR GILBOA

My Brother Was Silent

My brother came back from the field
In grey clothing,
And I was afraid my dream would be false
And began at once to count his wounds.
And my brother was silent.

Then I burrowed into the pockets of his tunic
And found a dressing with a dried stain,

And on a crumpled postcard his girl's name
Beneath a picture of some poppies.
And my brother was silent.

And I undid his bundle
And took out his things, memory after memory.
Hurray, my brother, my heroic brother,
Look, I've found your symbols!
Hurray, my brother, my heroic brother,
I'll shout your praises!
And my brother was silent.
And my brother was silent.

And his blood cried out of the ground.

translated by A. C. Jacobs

ÁGNES GERGELY
Sign on my Door Jamb

IN MEMORIAM MY FATHER

I do not cherish memories
and those I have I do not safeguard.
I do not seek forgotten graveyards.
Bio-chemistry doesn't move me.

Yet at times like this towards November
as fog-damped windows seal my room
and I gasp for air and long for relief,
I sense your invisible rise
as from the waters of the mind
and odd gestures of yours re-emerge.

I sense your long and nervous fingers
arranging a thermos flask and pocket knife
with the Bible and warm underclothes
and an old can opener in the gaping
green knapsack; and under the weightless load
you can carry, I sense your back's surprise.

I sense your departure, elegant tramp, from the house:
you'd never go away, you just set out,
and look back laughing, aged thirty-eight years,
and you nod and you gesture, *I'll soon return*
(tomorrow would have been your birthday)
while your tears dribble inwards whining
and you wave – and how you wave!

Sign on my door jamb, you've remained;
the bars, the bridge, the sludgy road,
the gorging of grass, the fatal empty weakness
are only freak inventions of the mind;
for I have lied, I often see you
beneath the stifling, low November sky;
you set out with me, you breathe, and your tears
I let your tears go dribbling down my throat;
and where it had fallen, the thin
cigarette struck from your mouth
has burned on a star ever since.

translated by Thomas Land

ZBIGNIEW HERBERT

The Rain

When my older brother
came back from the war
he had a little silver star on his forehead
and under the star
an abyss

a splinter of shrapnel
hit him at Verdun
or perhaps at Grünwald
(he didn't remember the details)

he talked a lot
in many languages
but most of all he liked
the language of history

until losing breath
he called to his dead comrades under the ground
Roland Jones Hannibal

he shouted
that this is the last crusade
soon Carthage will fall
and then sobbing confessed
that Napoleon doesn't like him

we watched
him become paler
his senses abandoned him
slowly he was turning into a monument

into musical shells of ears
entered a stone forest

the skin of his face
was fastened
with two blind dry
buttons of eyes

all he had left
was touch

what stories
he told with his hands
in the right he had romances
in the left soldier's memories

they took my brother
and carried him out of town

he returns now every autumn
thin and quiet
he doesn't want to enter the house
he knocks at the window for me to come out

we walk on the streets
and he tells me
unbelievable tales
touching my face
with blind fingers of weeping

translated by John Carpenter and Bogdana Carpenter

RACHEL KORN

Child, Say Your Confession

Today my mother came into my dream,
the prayer book in her hand,
with a moistened finger found the page and demanded:
Child. Say your confession. This is the time.

Nor was I surprised
that we stood looking down
at my last prayer.

My mother had three children.
Their heads were blond and chestnut-brown,
and all their eyes were dark as beer.

The younger two, her sons,
have joined her.
One, like her, with a German bullet
in the centre of his heart.
The other swam into the sky
in the black fumes of the crematorium.

Now she was calling
her eldest, her only daughter, home,
calling, calling, calling:
Child. This is the time. Say your confession.

The dark letters on the page
led me to the border
that we cross only once.

I broke from my last hour
like the branch of a tired tree,
my presence here
a fading dream.

Within me, stillness,
sunset deep in thought,
and only a waning ray of light – a narrow path –
to take my sorrow to the shore.

I felt terror,
yet
as if suddenly set free,
the longing to cling to this moment
I'd carried in me all my years.

There was no one to call me back,
no one longing after me.
No one to see me go.

My only witnesses, my lips,
tried to carry up to God
a shy childish smile I'd smiled long ago,
as if it were my last secret:

I said the prayer,
words on a yellowed piece of paper:
Dear Lord,
I am about to stand before you
with all my woe –

And I was ready.

And then suddenly in me or above me
was a voice that seemed sharpened on a whetstone;
'You haven't written all that you must,'

it said, and it tore me back into life
like a judge more just and more demanding,
sentencing an eternal debtor
to new effort and stumbling,
sin and forgiveness.

No one knew that I'd been gone.
Or that I'd returned.
And my waking to the new day
was hard and cruel –
There was no one waiting for me here.

translated by Seymour Levitan

NELLY SACHS

Chorus of the Rescued

We, the rescued,
From whose hollow bones death had begun to whittle his flutes,
And on whose sinews he had already stroked his bow –
Our bodies continue to lament
With their mutilated music.
We, the rescued,
The worms of fear still feed on us.
Our constellation is buried in dust.
We, the rescued,
Beg you:
Show us your sun, but gradually.
Lead us from star to star, step by step.
Be gentle when you teach us to live again.
Lest the song of a bird,
Or a pail being filled at the well,
Let our badly sealed pain burst forth again
and carry us away –
We beg you:
Do not show us an angry dog, not yet –
It could be, it could be
That we will dissolve into dust –
Dissolve into dust before your eyes.

For what binds our fabric together?
We whose breath vacated us,
Whose soul fled to Him out of that midnight
Long before our bodies were rescued
Into the ark of the moment.
We, the rescued,
We press your hand
We look into your eye –
But all that binds us together now is leave-taking,
The leave-taking in the dust
Binds us together with you.

translated by Michael Hamburger

NELLY SACHS

Chorus of the Orphaned

We orphans
We lament in the world:
Our branch has been cut down
And thrown into the fire –
Kindling was made of our protectors –
We orphans lie stretched out on the fields of loneliness.
We orphans
We lament to the world:
At night our parents play hide and seek –
From behind the black folds of night
Their faces gaze at us,
Their mouths speak:
Kindling we were in a woodcutter's hand –
But our eyes have become angel eyes
And regard you,
Through the black folds of night
They penetrate –
We orphans
We lament to the world:
Stones have become our playthings,

Stones have faces, father and mother faces
They wilt not like flowers, nor bite like beasts –
And burn not like tinder when tossed into the oven –
We orphans we lament to the world:

World, why have you taken our soft mothers from us
And the fathers who say: My child, you are like me!
We orphans are like no one in this world any more!
O world
We accuse you!

translated by Michael Hamburger

SALVATORE QUASIMODO

On the Branches of the Willows

And how could we have sung
with the foreign foot on our heart,
among the dead abandoned in the squares
on the grass set hard with ice, at the lamb-like
cry of children, at the black howl
of the mother advancing on her son
crucified on the telegraph pole?
On the branches of the willows, as a vow,
our poets' lyres were hanging,
swinging just a little in the dismal wind

translated by Geoff Page and Loredana Nardi-Ford

VIII

'For dreams are licensed as
they never were'

SÁNDOR CSOÓRI

The First Moments of Resurrection

The dog sat there on the manure pile,
covered with wounds and chaff of straw.
Enveloped by the stinking smell of Gehenna
sat the dog. The Easter bells pealed
for his wounds – ding-dong, ding-dong.
Wasps crawled out of the walls
of murdered buildings.
Nobody believed
that we had been resurrected!

The light-fingered survivors began
to undress the last dead of the war:
off came the helmets, the boots, the thick socks.
Off the pea jackets.
It looked as if mothers were peeling
grimy clothes off their drunken sons.
My God! What happened to you,
you hoodlum, you pig, my love!
Look at your sprung Adam's apple.
Your sweet head is bloody!

A southern breeze grazed me;
my fingertips bloomed in the barnyard of death.
I saw the unconquerable hen—
who lived only for the corn.
She struggled, as if possessed,
with the untied shoelaces of the dead.
She pulled and tugged, pecking in the mixture
of mud, hair and empty cartridge.
She all but soared, drunk with good fortune.
having collared the longest spring worm
in the world!

translated by Nicholas Kolumban

ISTVAN VAS

from *The Grand Finale*

February dawn spread across the sky.
Today at last we can cross over to Pest!
We cannot, though,
If the ice on the Danube won't let us go,
I thought, and just as the thought took
Hold of me, the neighbourhood shook.
I was about to doze off again
When I began to hear
The sound of gunfire and rockets
Mounting, drawing near.
No, that cannot be—
The siege of Buda starting once more?
And then a bang from the second floor—
The Russians are packing:
The half-light and the cold are hard—
And everything on the move—
Horses, carts, automobiles.
Like children we plead: 'Please don't go!'
'But we've got to go!
The Germans are breaking out of the Castle,
They're almost here!
We're leaving but not for long,
We'll be back – do not fear!'

The bang, the rattle increased outside;
Within us silence opened wide;
In our hearts, our room, the cold spread.
A scene bordering on madness:
Listening, the huge Academy courtyard
Across the way
Yawns wide.
Panic grows inside
Us: silence,
Mounting fear.

And what if the Germans come back here,
And Mrs Leitgeb reports us again.

. . .

While we still can,
We munch some bread,
Sit in a circle; the women smile,
The men stare glumly all the while.
The window rattles, the sun shines:
Across the room a bullet whines,
Until, weary of its flight,
It zings into the stove, whizzing right
Between Géza and me,
Between Mari and Gyöngyi.

We jump to our feet: the shadows
Of helmets in the distant courtyard move over the snow:

. . .

Three Russian soldiers appear.
They approach, jumping, ducking,
Cold afternoon sun flashing on their colourful persons—
Not on their helmets but on
The fur above
The green, yellow, and red
Of the caps on their heads.

These are the Sons of the Wondrous East,
Embodiment of a folktale past
And a dream
Future, and nearer they come.
One crawls below the window
And their Tommy guns rattle
Toward the place where moments ago
The messenger of doom stared up from the snow.

The man at the window can feel,
Through the winter landscape, the smell
Of smoke.
Heavy steps on the wooden stair;
We listen in fear,
Hoping. Three flamelike figures
Burst through the door.
Love, bravery, victory
Flash from each eye,
The light of the lovely war.

. . .

How many years has it been since then? What keeps me going still
Is having witnessed this grand finale.
Having seen how the big lie ended,
Having seen men
Take the mechanized monster
And tear it to shreds—
Having seen the infection-spreading flag
Sink into the mud,
Having seen what seemed iron and steel
Crumble like clay.

translated by William Jay Smith

ANNA AKHMATOVA

From the Plane

I

Over thousands of *versts*, over thousands of miles,
over thousands of kilometres,
salt lay, grass rustled,
the cedar groves loomed.
As though for the first time in my whole life
I was looking at my homeland,

I realised it's all mine –
my body, and my soul.

II

I will mark that day with a white stone,
when, outstripping the sun, I flew
to meet victory head on
and sang of the victory I knew.

III

The grass of the spring
aerodrome rustles underfoot.
Home, real homecoming!
How new yet familiar everything is
and how good the heart feels!
and the head spins sweetly
in the fresh May thunder.
Moscow the Victorious!

May 1944
translated by Richard McKane

RUTH PITTER

Victory Bonfire

It is a legend already: a wide wide stubble,
Barley-stubble, a hundred pale acres,
With a mountain of straw stacked in the middle, towering, looming,
Big as a small hotel. They had ploughed round it
Thirty furrows for a firebreak,
Right away from the house, outbuildings, stackyard,
Right away from the coppice, orchard, hedges:
And high-climbing boys had planted an image of Hitler
On the lonely summit, Adolf forlornly leering.

[221]

We made ourselves nests of straw on the edge of the stubble,
In a sweet September twilight, a full moon rising
Far out on the blond landscape, as if at sea,
And the mighty berg of straw was massive before us;
Barley-straw, full of weed-seeds, fit only for burning;
House and barn and low buildings little and hull-down yonder.
People were wandering in, the children noisy, a rumour of fireworks
Rife among them; the infants never had seen any.
We sat attentive. In their straw nests, the smallest
Piled themselves lovingly on each other. Now the farmer's four young
        ones
Stalked over the ploughed strip, solemn with purpose.

Wisps of smoke at the four corners –
Tongues of flame on the still blue evening,
And she's away! . . . A pause, a crackle, a roar!
Sheets of orange flame in a matter of seconds –
And in a matter of minutes – hypnotized minutes –
Vast caverns of embers, volcanoes gushing and blushing,
Whitening wafts on cliffs and valleys of hell,
Quivering cardinal-coloured glens and highlands,
Great masses panting, pulsating, lunglike and scarlet,
Fireballs, globes of pure incandescence
Soaring up like balloons, formal and dreadful,
Threatening the very heavens. The moon climbing
Shakes like a jelly through heated air – it's Hitler!
Look, look! Hitler's ghost! Cheering and screaming –
Some not quite sure how they like it. Now Daddy Foster
Springs a surprise – he's touched off some rockets. O murder!
Knife-edged shrieks from half the young entry!
Buzz-saw howls from the wartime vintage,
For a rocket can only be a V2,
A firecracker a thermite bomb. O hang Daddy Foster!
(So mighty in energy, mighty in influence,
Able to get unobtainable fireworks through Business Contacts.)
There are mothers retreating, taking their weepers with them.
With jangled nerves they execrate Daddy Foster,
Giving him little glory of Business Contacts,
And wondering how long it will be before their infants
Are quiet in their beds. And fireworks will be a lot cheaper

Before they or theirs will squander a sixpence on them.
Little girls from the farm bring lapfuls of apples
From the orchard yonder, picked in the moonlight.
They know the kinds by the shape of the trunks,
So often they've climbed there. These are the earlies,
Worcester Pearmain and Miller's Seedling,
Hard and red in one skirt, soft, milky-pale in the other.
There are drinks, sandwiches, ice-cream out of the baskets,
The glow of the gleed on our faces, and elsewhere
Autumn chill creeping. Into the straw we burrow,
Murmuring and calling, getting colder and sleepier,
And the awns of the barley are working into our souls –
(*Troppo mustachio*, says the Eyetye prisoner)
And the fire is falling, and high and haughty the moon
Shows us our homeward path. Good-nights, then silence:
And the mole-cricket clinks alone, and the stubbles are vacant,
Only blushing and whitening embers left fading and falling.

ISTVÁN VAS

Boccherini's Tomb

Shall we go there, too? Whatever for? Another half-Gothic
Small checkered church whose inside has been ruined.
Sub-baroque. We're lucky that it's dark.
Let's get away from here. But wait a moment, there's something white
    showing over there,
A huge nose, a vaulted head, set in the wall. And a lute below?
Well, let's have a look. It's Boccherini's tomb.
How did it get here? He was born in Lucca, of course,
Though he lived in Madrid. You may remember
The Madrid Guard on record.

But that wasn't the first thing of his I'd heard.
It was rather late in my life before I'd even heard his name,
And the place and time were rather strange.
Gödöllö, the school gymnasium. There were a hundred of us.
Or more. And a little rotten straw.

The only place you could go out to was the yard.
Where the snow was deep. We could wash in it,
But then (do you remember? It was a cold winter) it froze,
And they urinated all over it . . . but, you recall, once
You got in and bribed the guard and took me out to wash.
You can imagine what we were like after two weeks. But I
Wasn't the only poet in the gymnasium.
Tom Fool was there, too, who not long before
Had been writing Fascist articles, but since his luck had worsened,
All he talked about was who should hang.
And there was another, who later celebrated the hefty little leader
In such artful poems; but at times he was a real
Poet – you had to admit that – and he was also
A good mate in trouble and behaved wonderfully well—
Threatening to boot the contaminated Jews
Who sang one of the German soldier songs inside.
But they weren't the ones who consoled me; it was a red-haired printer
Who put up with all that happened, always gay and sarcastic.
It was he who whistled the Boccherini minuet all day,
That mocking ironical pizzicato minuet,
Which made fun of everything including
The minuet itself. When we were inoculated
Against typhoid and the Medical Officer remarked
That we were all pretty dirty, even then
He hissed it in my ear; and whenever I was really downcast,
He began to hum it especially for me, and that
Restored my courage and I laughed again.
Then, as you know, I soon got out of there;
I've always been something of an exception. He went up to the front,
From which he managed to return, God knows how;
He joined the Party, but I haven't heard anything about him for a
        long time;
I'm not even sure he didn't emigrate on one occasion or another.

But now here in the dark church I remember him
And in thought bend my knees not to Francis,
The gentle, poor, super-poet, the saint,
But to the mocking minuet, Boccherini's pizzicatos.
And to Andor Rottman (now I can safely put down his name:
He turned it into Hungarian later, to what I've forgotten.)

And to C., who lived there, near the Gödöllö gymnasium,
Something I didn't know, not knowing him at the time,
But later, when things became even worse for me, he hid me at his
    place.
And to A., who also saved my life
Without having been asked to, rewarded only by my disapproval.
And to K., the unlaurelled outstanding poet whom
I sent to you on a secret mission, and who, entering,
Clicked his heels: 'L. K., Secretary to the Minister'.
That's how he introduced himself to the Commander
Of the Desemitizing Unit, who was armed to the teeth;
Not to mention a number of women, whose names
I shall not put down, since they would not like to appear together on
    this page,
In other words, to everyone in that dark church who then
Helped guard my sanity.

translated by William Jay Smith

LOUIS SIMPSON

I Dreamed that in a City Dark as Paris

I dreamed that in a city dark as Paris
I stood alone in a deserted square.
The night was trembling with a violet
Expectancy. At the far edge it moved
And rumbled; on that flickering horizon
The guns were pumping colour in the sky.

There was the Front. But I was lonely here,
Left behind, abandoned by the army.
The empty city and the empty square
Was my inhabitation, my unrest.
The helmet with its vestige of a crest,
The rifle in my hands, long out of date,
The belt I wore, the trailing overcoat

and hobnail boots, were those of a *poilu*.
I was the man, as awkward as a bear.

Over the rooftops where cathedrals loomed
In speaking majesty, two aeroplanes
Forlorn as birds, appeared. Then growing large,
The German *Taube* and the *Nieuport Scout*,
They chased each other tumbling through the sky,
Till one streamed down on fire to the earth.

These wars have been so great, they are forgotten
Like the Egyptian dynasts. My confrere
In whose thick boots I stood, were you amazed
To wander through my brain four decades later
As I have wandered in a dream through yours?

The violence of waking life disrupts
The order of our death. Strange dreams occur,
For dreams are licensed as they never were.

BORIS SLUTSKY

In a non-sleeper

In a non-sleeper, without reserved places,
one passenger sleeps restlessly, as if
in a city under occupation, his
bundle kept under his side continuously.

Yet theft is a thing of the past, surely
all robbers have been locked away.
Just go to sleep, and if you don't fall off
your seat, there's time to scan your dreams enjoyably.

But he lies awkwardly drawn up
                                          and cramped
his fingers clenched into a fist;
he sleeps as if his bundle must
contain important secret information.

In here there's light and heating, even
an unreserved carriage isn't so bad:
but things that happened once in
other times than these persist, and
cast their shadows on his lips.

Yes, the man sleeps as if still in the war:
uneasily
    as though afraid to make
some terrible mistake
    while he is sleeping.

translated by Elaine Feinstein

JUN OKAMOTO
Under The Hazy, Blossom-laden Sky

Under the hazy, blossom-laden sky
The city sprawls, its gaping wounds exposed:
The streets due for a surgical operation,
Canals gathering pitch and filth,
Bridges with their concrete peeling away.

Under the hazy, blossom-laden sky
Cranes moving,
Drain-pipes lined up,
Truck after truck
Carrying dirt, rubbish, mud,
The burnt-out, festering hulks of war.

Dark caverns in the streets:
On the canal bed, submerged groans and sighs
Of those who will not surface:
Methane gushing up.

In the city with these clogged wounds
International streets will appear soon,
Rows of gay shops will grow,
Tempting goods will brighten the windows.

Under the hazy, blossom-laden sky,
New building goes on.

Our ears tuned to the detonations under the hazy,
      blossom-laden sky,
We pray
That the fire-rain never again fall on the world.

translated by Geoffrey Bownas and Anthony Thwaite

GÜNTER EICH
Geometrical Place

We have sold our shadow,
it hangs on a wall in Hiroshima,
a transaction we knew nothing of,
from which, embarrassed, we rake in interest.

And, dear friends, drink my whiskey,
I won't be able to find the tavern any more,
where my bottle stands
with its monogram,
old proof of a clear conscience.

I didn't put my penny in the bank
when Christ was born
but I've seen the grandchildren
of dogs trained to herd people
on the hills near the Danube School,
and they stared at me.

And I want, like the people of Hiroshima,
to see no more burnt skin,
I want to drink and sing songs,
to sing for whiskey,
and to stroke the dogs, whose grandfathers
sprang at people
in quarries and barbed wire.

You, my shadow,
on the bank at Hiroshima,
I want to visit you with all the dogs
now and then
and drink to you
to the prosperity of our accounts.

The museum is being demolished,
in front of it
I will slip to you
behind your railing,
behind your smile – our cry for help—
and we'll suit each other again,
your shoes into mine
precise
to the second.

translated by Stuart Friebert

JAROSLAV SEIFERT

Never Again

A hundred houses were in ruins,
nearly a thousand had been damaged
by aerial bombs.
No, I didn't count them myself.
I worked my way through the rubble
and circumnavigated the craters.
They were frightening
like gaping gates to fiery hell.

Speedily they cleared away the debris
but it was three days before
they broke into the little house
in Šverma Street,
the house of Mr Hrnčíř.
The whole family was dead.

Only the rooster, that fighting cock
whom the Apostle Peter did not
greatly love,
alone had saved himself.
Over the bodies of the dead he'd climbed
onto a pile of rubble.

He looked about the scene of the disaster
and spread his wings
to shake the heavy dust
from his golden feathers.

And I repeated softly to myself
what I had found written
in letters of grief and in letters of pain
upon the faces of the Kralupy people.

And into that silence of death
I screamed in a loud voice,
so loud the war should hear it:
Never again, war!

The rooster looked at me
with its black beady eye
and burst into horrible laughter.
He laughed at me
and at my pointless screaming.
Besides, he was a bird
and sided with the planes.
The bastard!

translated by Ewald Osers

HOWARD NEMEROV
The Bacterial War

Above all, not by violence –
We fought without brutality
And only test-tubes could incense

Heroes to their mortality.
The public and obedient saints,
The right to serve their single pride,
Lined up with all their documents,
Enlisted and inhaled and died.

Encounters with the enemy
Were frowned upon by adjutants;
Soldiers instead would fight to be
Strangled by simple ambience,
And breath was all the bravery
Of those without the uniform
Who did not hold Thermopylae
Against the microscopic worm.

Not guilt but total innocence
The outcome of this holy war –
Not so much man's was the offence
But it was nature's so much more.
The sons of man with perfect sense
Thereon attacked both time and space,
And sought to kill the present tense
And square the round world's grievous face.

HOWARD NEMEROV

Redeployment

They say the war is over. But water still
Comes bloody from the taps, and my pet cat
In his disorder vomits worms which crawl
Swiftly away. Maybe they leave the house.
These worms are white, and flecked with the cat's blood.

The war may be over. I know a man
Who keeps a pleasant souvenir, he keeps
A soldier's dead blue eyeballs that he found
Somewhere – hard as chalk, and blue as slate.
He clicks them in his pocket while he talks.

And now there are cockroaches in the house,
They get slightly drunk on DDT,
Are fast, hard, shifty – can be drowned but not
Without you hold them under quite some time.
People say the Mexican kind can fly.

The end of the war. I took it quietly
Enough. I tried to wash the dirt out of
My hair and from under my fingernails,
I dressed in clean white clothes and went to bed.
I heard the dust falling between the walls.

GÜNTER GRASS

Kleckerburg

Aimed questions, foresight well aligned
lifelong the backsight will demand:
When I had left the witness box,
stood up in court, before a wall,
where frontiers contravert the rivers,
twelve thousand feet above the smog,
at home, the barber breathed upon
his mirror, and his finger wrote:
Born when? And – out with it – born where?
   It lies to the north-east, west of,
   and still can feed photographers.
   Its name was this and now is that.
   There lived until, from then on lived.
   I spell: its name was Wrzeszcz before.
   The house still stands, but the façade.
   The graveyard, which has ceased to be.
   Where fences were now anyone.
   Such gothic things does God think up.
   For once again at great expense.
   I counted gables, none was missing:
   The Middle Ages catch us up.
   Only that statue with the tail

has ridden off now, has gone west.
And every station signal also asks;
for when, between small shells, I built sand castles,
when I unearthed a tombstone outside Brenntau,
when I turned over papers in the archives
and in five languages the form in the hotel:
Born when and where, block letters please, born why?
yapped for the answers, my ball pen confessed:
  It was when *Rentenmarks* were current.
  Here, by the Mottlau, a small tributary,
  where Forster roared, Hirsch Fajngold held his tongue,
  where I wore out the soles of my first pair
  of shoes, and being old enough to speak
  learned how to stammer: sand, all clammy
  for making castles, until my childhood grail
  gothically towered and collapsed.
  That was some twenty years after Verdun;
  came thirty years of respite, till my sons
  made me a father; stable smells
  talk in this lilt, collector's mania
  when stories, butterflies I impaled
  and fished for words that cat-like trembled
  on rafts of driftwood washed ashore,
  gave birth to twelve, all grey and blind.
Born when? And where? Block letters please. And why?
Those questions I have dragged around,
sunk in the Rhine, buried near Hildesheim;
but divers found them and in dragging nets
flotsam and jetsam rose, were brought to light.
  Beechnuts and amber, sherbet fizz,
  this pen-knife and this transfer picture,
  piece of a piece, ship tonnage figures,
  buttons and coins and minute hands,
  for every square a bag of wind.
  To confidence tricks I'm driven by
  my treasure trove, lost property office.
  The smells, the thresholds trodden down,
  debts never paid, small batteries
  happy in torches, only torches,
  and names that are no more than names;

Elfriede Broschke, Siemoneit,
Guschnerus, Lusch and Heinz Stanowski;
and Chodowiecki, Schopenhauer
were born there too. Born when? Born why?
Yes, I was always good at history.
Ask me about the plagues and price increases.
I'll rattle off peace treaties like Hail Marys,
masters of orders, Swedish war,
and know the Jagellons by heart,
and all the churches, from St John's
to Holy Trinity, red brick.
    Who still asks where? My intonation
is Baltic, wily, warm as rooms.
What says the Baltic? Blubb, pfff, pshsh ...
In German, Polish: Blubb, pfff, pshsh ...
But when I asked the functionaries
at the assembly-weary, coach-
and-special-train-fed gathering
of eastern refugees at Hanover,
they had forgotten what the Baltic says
and made the Atlantic Ocean roar;
I kept insisting: Blubb, pfff, pshsh ...
So: Hit him! Kill him! all yelled out,
he's turned his back on human rights,
on pensions, on his native city,
on compensations, restitutions,
just listen to his intonation:
That's not the Baltic, that's high treason.
Put screws on him and make him talk,
get wheels and tongs and pokers, blind him,
and stretch his memory on the rack.
We want his answer: when and where.
Not on the Straw Dyke, nor in Merchants' Meadows,
nor yet in Pepper Town – would that I had
been born between great store lofts on the Holm! –
Near the small Streissbach, by the Rifle Range
it happened, and today the street
in Polish is called Lelewela – only
the number left of the door remains, remains.
And sand, for castles, clammy, muddy: grail ...

At Kleckerburg was born, west of.
It lies to the northwest, south of.
The light there changes much more than.
The seagulls are not seagulls, but.
And there the Milch, a Vistula tributary,
honeyed and many-bridged flowed by.
   Baptized and vaccinated, schooled, confirmed.
   Bomb splinters, meanwhile, were my toys.
   And I grew up, was reared between
   the Holy Ghost and Hitler's photograph.
   Ships' sirens echo in my ears,
   lopped sentences and wind-blown cries,
   a few sound churchbells, rifle fire
   and Baltic snatches: Blubb, pfff, pshsh . . .

translated by Michael Hamburger

JOHN CIARDI

To Lucasta, About That War

  A long winter from home the gulls blew
     on their brinks, the tankers slid
     over the hump where the wolf packs hid
     like voodoo talking, the surf threw
     bundles with eyes ashore. I did
     what booze brought me, and it wasn't you.

  I was almost bored. I watched and told time
     as enforced, a swag-man
     under the clock. The bloat-bags ran
     wet from nowhere, selling three-for-a-dime
     and nobody buying. Armies can
     type faster than men die, I'm

  told, and can prove. Didn't I find
     time there, and more, to count
     all, triplicate, and still walk guard-mount
     on the gull- and drum-wind
     over the hump? I did, and won't
     deny several (or more) pig-blind

alleys with doors, faces, dickers,
   which during, the ships slid
   over the humps where the packs hid.
   And talking voodoo and snickers
   over the edge of their welts, I did
   what I could with (they called them) knickers;

and it was goddam good,
   and not bad either. It
   was war (they called it) and it lit
   a sort of skyline somehow in the blood,
   and I typed the dead out a bit
   faster than they came, or anyone should,

and the gulls blew high on their brinks,
   and the ships slid, and the surf threw,
   and the army initialled, and you
   were variously, and straight and with kinks,
   raped, fondled, and apologized to –
   which is called (as noted) war. And it stinks.

JAMES K. BAXTER

Returned Soldier

The boy who volunteered at seventeen
At twenty-three is heavy on the booze.
Strafed in the desert and bombed out in Crete—
With sore dark eyes and hardened by the heat
Entitled now to call himself a man
And in the doll's-house walk with death-at-ease;
The Cairo women, cobbers under sand
A death too great for dolls to understand.

Back to a city bed or station hut
At maelstrom centre falling through the night
To dreams where deeper than El Alamein
A buried childhood stirs with leaves and flowers
Remembered girls, the blurred and bitter waters.
Wakes to the midnight rafters and the rain.

JAMES DICKEY

The War Wound

It wounded well – one time and
A half: once with instant blood and again
Reinfecting blackly, years later. Now all
  Is calm at the heel of my hand

Where I grabbed, in a bellied-
in airplane, and caught the dark glass
Offered once in a lifetime by
  The brittle tachometer.

Moons by the thousands
Have risen in all that time; I hold
The healed half-moon of that night.
  I tell it to shine as still

As it can in the temperate flesh
That never since has balled into a fist,
To hover on nylon guitar strings
  Like the folk-moon itself;

I tell it to burn like a poison
When my two children threaten themselves,
Wall-walking, or off the deep end
  Of a county swimming pool,

And with thousands of moons
Coming over me year after year,
I lie with it well under cover,
  The war of the millions,

Through glass ground under
Heel twenty-one years ago
Concentrating its light on my hand,
  Small, but with world-fury.

IOAN ALEXANDRU

The End of the War

When I came into the world the war was endin',
Last orders were shot. On field
Last cannons were hung by their shadows.
In our house presents were shared.

'First to you, John,' said the War to father, from the corner of
        the table,
'Because you have served me so faithfully
I hand you this wooden leg.
Wear it in memory of me, and good health to you.
It's sturdy from the trunk of an old oak;
When you die the woods will rock you
Like a brother in the summits of their eyes.
Your right hand, because it has no book learning anyway,
I wrenched from your elbow and have given it to the earth
To teach it to write.

'For you, Maria,' said the War to my mother –
'Because you watered my horses with your tears
And left two sons on the battlefield
To polish my boots, and brought up
Two maidens with whom I've spent my nights,
Look, I'll give you this beautiful bunch of wakeful nights,
As well as this empty house without a roof.

'To you, George, son of Peter from over the hill, –
For those two hazel eyes, you say you had,
Look, I give you possession of all the boundaries of darkness,
So you can harvest them, you and your wife
Forever.

'For the village I leave only forty orphans
Under six months, ten empty houses and the others in ruins,
Also, the sky towards sunset, half-burned.
The tower without bells; eight women in the cemetery
Hung with heads to the ground, and twenty horses dead from
        the neighbour's farm.

[238]

'For you, just born, because we don't know each other very well,
I leave the cow's udder dry,
The plum trees burned alive in the garden,
The eye of the well, dead,
And may the sky feed you on its stars.
And I baptize you in the name of the Lord.'

translated by Andrea Deletant and Brenda Walker

LILY BRETT

People Weeping

I was born
in the middle
of a provisional government

allies
willing
to help us

my earliest memories
are of
people weeping

we were
newly-arrived prisoners
recently-survived victims

we were
women still searching
we were men still hoping

we were
others
who had given up

we were
forgotten lovers
and lost fathers

we were
left-over daughters
and missing mothers

we were
awkward
and uncomfortable

angry
restless guests
in Germany

lists of the dead
and the living
were posted daily

there were
no lists
of those of us

stuck
between
lists.

LILY BRETT

My Mother's Friend

My mother
had a schoolfriend
she shared the war with

my mother
looked after her friend
in the ghetto

she laid her out
as though she was dead
and the Gestapo overlooked her

in Auschwitz
she fed her friend snow
when she was burning with typhoid

and when
the Nazis
emptied Stuthof

they threw
the inmates
on to boats in the Baltic

and tried
to drown
as many as they could

my mother
and her friend
survived

in
Bayreuth
after the war

my mother's friend
patted my cheeks
and curled my curls

and hurled herself
from the top
of a bank.

ÁGNES NEMES NAGY

Storm

A shirt blows across the field.
Freed from a clothes-horse
at the height of an Equinox,
stumbling now above Saint Swithin's Grass
it is the bodiless dance
of a veteran.

And there they go, the sheets
running under the recoil of lightning
in battalion manœuvres
even as they flee – flags, sheets,
a top-sail, a rag – each
ripped to its own hissing sound
on the open green field
diving and rising
their movement unveils
the winding sheets of mass-graves.

Without moving, I step
outside my contour,
a somewhat more transparent runner
body taut behind among them
like a half-wit whose birds have flown
like a naked tree whose birds have flown
calling them back with my beckoning arms–
And now they fall.
And with a motion white-winged, wide,
the entire flock takes wing as one,
takes wing like an unmoving image
takes wing like the bodily resurrection,
eternity called up
from the water, at the crack of a gun.

Nothing left in the field but that beckon
and the dark green colour
of the grass. A pond.

translated by Hugh Maxton

ERICH FRIED

Transformation

My girl-friends turn slowly
over three or four weeks
or quickly over night
into my aunts and old cousins

I see them chew anxiously
at their dentures
and with gouty fingers dry
the spittle from their faces

With cases and bundles
they arrive in Theresienstadt
They fumble for their glasses
as they fall from the window

Curled up in bed
they turn to come to attention
so as to be spared
when they weed out the sick

When I kiss them in the morning
I see their bluish tint
piled high
washed clean with garden-hoses

of shit and vomited slime
ready for transport
from the gas-chamber
to the cremation oven

translated by Stuart Hood

EUGEN JEBELEANU

Lidice

Do you remember? . . .
                      It was winter.
Snowflakes were slowly drifting down,
swan's-down pillowed on the cold air,
trembling, uncertain of what lay there
beneath them on the hard ground.

We had left Prague behind us in the morning,
its steeples melting in the mist;
the car crossed fields flat as the tray in the warm parlour
where we had stolen an urban rest.
To the right shone Morawska Ostrava.

We were going to Lidice. None of us
asked questions. We looked through the window
at brown villages and the blue forest
as they, too, flew out of our sight.

The war had ended. There, where yesterday
the tank had passed, now there were miners;
over the struggling woods slow clouds of smoke
rose from the peaceful furnaces into the air.

We were rushing towards Lidice, when . . . suddenly
the car left the road, pushing aside the smoke
and snow, crossed the field in high winter,
made a small detour, then stopped.

'What is it?' I asked. 'Why have we stopped,
here, where there is nothing?'
(We were going to Lidice.)
'Here,' said the guide, 'here is the village.'

We looked for as far as the eye could see
at the snow weaving now soft fabrics

[244]

with which to mantle the ground that was
desert, scorched trees, ravens . . . and Lidice.
And in all this nothing . . . a small museum.

We went in, the Czech, you and I. He said:
'This is all that is left now.'
We bent towards the far wall
in a gesture that might have been a bow.

In a glass case, gathered together in a box,
a handful of tiny, charred things:
a pen, a piece of money, a rusty leash,
a whistle blown up by the dynamite,
a doorknob, some maimed spectacles
mended with wire, for an old man's eyes,
a black, brass wedding-ring,
a mattock, a thimble, a frame. . . .

And in a corner, another case,
with two small skates and a doll. . . .
My fingers found the tears in my eyes,
but I did not want to cry. . . . It was snowing.

I wanted to go out. I looked at you,
but the small skates kept me back. . . .
It was snowing hard, now . . . how brightly
they would shine over the hard ground.

Our guide was past weeping. He said nothing;
all we could do was to take his hand
in ours, building a high wall of hatred
against the past, and this kept the wind away
from our hearts; we turned to watch
with the wind from the stone window,
beyond which were the snows and the barren land,
beyond which were the dream fields of grain.

But the sky wept. And the skates did not move.
There was just time enough to wonder if we had arrived
(we were going to Lidice), and it was cold on the ground
as the warm snow fell, softly, about our eyes.

translated by Roy MacGregor Hastie

SÁNDOR CSOÓRI

Remembering an Old Street

Little crooked street:
Discarded melon slice.
Black seeds are your cobbles.
You are covered with flies.

Your synagogue's face:
A stuffed heifer's face.

The earlocks of your small Jews are curly,
Their skinny hands flat noodles roll,
They only have their god, no department store,
They came riding the winds from Bethlehem.

Who has seen Moses with beard of oakum?
He comes by here every night;
He draws water from the stones,
He draws water from the walls,
And by dawn your pavement is a muddy sight.

My listlessness looks at you,
My pondering eyes glance back from here;
A little Jewish girl returns my greeting,
Her eyes are six-pointed stars of constant fear.

A straw flies up now, caught in air—
You! The living! Can you see?
The little Jewish girl's yellow bone
Flies into a yellow nullity.

It flies to mother: green gas in space,
It flies to father: lampshade on the moon,
It flies to brother: rectangular dry soap
In a shop window of the next world of hope.

Little street, little street, Europe's
Tiny poppy-seed street; death's footprint
Can you see in your black mud,
Despite your eyesight, weakening?

I am moving out, away from you, forever;
Leaving only my memories:
Your windmill trees will grind them up with ease,
And your birds will devour them.

translated by Andrew Feldmar

JERZY FICOWSKI
The Silence of the Earth

Time here is reckoned only by the woodpecker,
the cuckoo tells out the hours.

This way once people passed crying,
the juniper tugged at their coat flaps.

For years those shot have lain here
in the deep silence of the earth.

They do not break the branches of the trees,
faces do not sprout from boughs,

eyes do not burst from buds.

A cry does not shatter the view of wood,
the earth does not tear off the view of grasslands,
does not fling off its sheets of wild thyme

The lime-trees do not shut off their fragrance,
the grains are not afraid to grow,
the roads do not run off into the fields.

[247]

The roadside stones do not whine,
the smooth air does not crumble,
the wind breathes no sigh.

And they utter not a word
not a leaf nor a sandgrain

who are devoured by the roots of the pines.

translated by Keith Bosley and Krystyna Wandycz

SALVATORE QUASIMODO

Snow

The evening is coming down: once again you are leaving us,
dear images of earth, trees,
animals, the wretched wrapped
in the cloaks of soldiers, mothers
with their wombs made dry by tears.
The snow from the meadows lights us
like the moon. Oh these dead. Beat
on your foreheads, right through to the heart.
Someone at least should scream in the silence,
in this white circle of the buried.

translated by Geoff Page and Loredana Nardi-Ford

ZOLTÁN ZELK

And And

When I came into the room I saw
my murderer
chatting in a shell-shaped chair
sneaking dumbstruck through the walls
drenched in electric light—
How I pitied him! Does he remember,

he who killed? He reaches out his hand,
I take it and sit down beside him and
  how've you been Oh still alive and kicking
  it's twenty years well time does pass
  but we're still full of piss and vinegar
  in spite of troubles when it rains it pours
  in spite of dentures and a coronary and
and and
talking
and the needle scrapes the record
and coffee and sandwiches and drinks
and cigarettes and a few cigars
and sofa and bunk-bed and ticking full of straw
and blizzards and blighted appletrees
and forest fires and rivers flooding
and it's after midnight and the words drop off
and the guests put down their drinks
propping up the wall of night
that kept the world from crashing on them.

translated by Daniel Hoffman

DAN PAGIS

Draft of a Reparations Agreement

All right, gentlemen who cry blue murder as always,
nagging miracle-makers,
quiet!
Everything will be returned to its place,
paragraph after paragraph.
The scream back into the throat.
The gold teeth back to the gums.
The terror.
The smoke back to the tin chimney and further on and inside
back to the hollow of the bones,
and already you will be covered with skin and sinews and you
    will live,

look, you will have your lives back,
sit in the living room, read the evening paper.
Here you are. Nothing is too late.
As to the yellow star: immediately
it will be torn from your chest
and will emigrate

translated by Stephen Mitchell

ABBA KOVNER

On the Way

Mother and father are beginning to die inside me.
Thirty years after their deaths in the storm
they withdraw quietly from my rooms,
from my moments of grace.

I'm sure about it. Voices and words have stopped,
they're free now. They no longer visit
my house, but not because they are angry.
A living man must be on his own.

Somewhere father is getting up early,
walking around in his sandals, pretending
as usual he doesn't see how mother cries
as she knits a warm sweater for her son,
camped on the way in the night.

translated by Shirley Kaufmann

PRIMO LEVI

The Survivor

TO B.V.

Dopo di allora, ad ora incerta,
Since then, at an uncertain hour,
That agony returns:
And till my ghastly tale is told,
This heart within me burns.

Once more he sees his companions' faces
Livid in the first faint light,
Gray with cement dust,
Nebulous in the mist,
Tinged with death in their uneasy sleep.
At night, under the heavy burden
Of their dreams, their jaws move,
Chewing a nonexistent turnip.
'Stand back, leave me alone, submerged people,
Go away. I haven't dispossessed anyone,
Haven't usurped anyone's bread.
No one died in my place. No one.
Go back into your mist.
It's not my fault if I live and breathe,
Eat, drink, sleep and put on clothes.'

4 February 1984
translated by Ruth Feldman

ABBA KOVNER

from *My Little Sister*

You are silent.
But our mother used to light
a candle for the saving of her soul
every day.

The candles ran out in the ghetto, and the oxygen
in the bunker.
My mother kindled her soul
on all the seas.

Out mother mourned a daughter
who never came into the world.
From 1940 to 1948. The rest of her sons were cut down.
and she lamented them,
and she mourned my little sister
who never came into the world.

                                    — You who saw
everything.
You who saw us.
mother!
How mourn to our faces
someone
who never came into the world?

And mother stared at me for a while.
And she stared at me for a long while.
Until her lips parted to speak,
and she said, my son
— she was not privileged to see
the light of the day.

And she came close.
And she prepared the candle.
And her hand was holding
another wick.

no one will carry my mother's bier with me
no one will come close to my mother's bier with me
come to the vast plains
lead your eyes to the white river
it scoops out its channel and shoves
like the prow of a heavy
ship in the ice
and say with me
imi
imi

translated by Shirley Kaufmann

CZESŁAW MIŁOSZ

Dedication

You whom I could not save
Listen to me.
Try to understand this simple speech as I would be ashamed of another.

I swear, there is in me no wizardry of words.
I speak to you with silence like a cloud or a tree.

What strengthened me, for you was lethal.
You mixed up farewell to an epoch with the beginning of a new one,
Inspiration of hatred with lyrical beauty,
Blind force with accomplished shape.

Here is the valley of shallow Polish rivers. And an immense bridge
Going into white fog. Here is a broken city,
And the wind throws screams of gulls on your grave
When I am talking with you.

What is poetry which does not save
Nations or people?
A connivance with official lies,
A song of drunkards whose throats will be cut in a moment,
Readings for sophomore girls.
That I wanted good poetry without knowing it,
That I discovered, late, its salutary aim,
In this and only this I find salvation.

They used to pour on graves millet or poppy seeds
To feed the dead who would come disguised as birds.
I put this book here for you, who once lived
So that you should visit us no more.

1945
translated by the poet

PRIMO LEVI

For Adolf Eichmann

The wind runs free across our plains,
The live sea beats for ever at our beaches.
Man makes earth fertile, earth gives him flowers and fruits.
He lives in toil and joy; he hopes, fears, begets sweet
    offspring.

... And you have come, our precious enemy,
Forsaken creature, man ringed by death.
What can you say now, before our assembly?
Will you swear by a god? What god?
Will you leap happily into the grave?
Or will you at the end, like the industrious man
Whose life was too brief for his long art,
Lament your sorry work unfinished,
The thirteen million still alive?

Oh son of death, we do not wish you death.
May you live longer than anyone ever lived.
May you live sleepless five million nights,
And may you be visited each night by the suffering of
   everyone who saw,
Shutting behind him, the door that blocked the way back,
Saw it grow dark around him, the air fill with death.

20 July 1960
translated by Ruth Feldman

IX

'War is no longer declared but continued'

SALVATORE QUASIMODO

Man of My Time

You are still the one with stone and sling,
man of my time. You were in the cockpit there
with your vicious wings, with the sundials of death.
I have seen you in the carts of fire, at the scaffold
and the wheels of torture. I have seen you, it was you,
with your neat sciences persuaded to extermination,
without love, without Christ. You've killed again,
as always, as the fathers killed, as the animals
killed when first they saw you.
This blood smells like the day
when the brother said to the other brother
'Let us go into the fields'. And that echo, cold, tenacious,
has reached right down to you in your own day.
Forget, sons, the clouds of blood
risen from the earth, forget the fathers:
their tombs are going down in ashes, black birds and the wind
are covering their hearts.

translated by Geoff Page and Loredana Nardi-Ford

EVGENY VINOKUROV

Crusaders

Unswerving is the path he follows
Who burns with an inner flame . . .
The crusaders press on, taking
Each town for Jerusalem . . .
They slaughter, burn, trample and maim,
Seize the townsfolk, lead them captive off,
And afterwards, shrugging, exclaim:
'So, it wasn't the right one after all!'
But then, spying towers far away,

Again they lower their visors
Over their eyes. 'This time,' they say,
'There's no mistaking it.'

translated by A. Rudolf and D. Weissbort

TADEUSZ RÓŻEWICZ

Mars

A room

a family
of five or six

someone's reading a book
someone's looking at photographs
someone remembers the war
someone's falling asleep someone leaves
someone's dying in the silence
someone's drinking water
someone's breaking bread
Tommy writes the letter A
and draws a knight with a blue spur
someone's getting ready to go to the moon
someone's brought a rose a bird a fish
it's snowing
a bell tolls

Mars appears
his sword
fills the room
with fire

translated by Adam Czerniawski

SALVATORE QUASIMODO

The Soldiers Cry at Night

Neither the Cross nor childhood nor
Golgotha's hammer nor the memory
of an angel is enough to tear out
war. The soldiers cry
at night before dying, they are strong,
they fall at the feet of words
learned under the arms of life.
Love numbers the soldiers,
the nameless bursts of crying.

translated by Edwin Morgan

PRIMO LEVI

Epitaph

Oh you, passing by this hill – one
Among many – who mark this no longer solitary snow,
Hear my story. Stop for a few moments
Here where, dry-eyed, my comrades buried me,
Where, every summer, the gentle field-grass fed by me
Grows thicker and greener than elsewhere.
Killed by my companions for no small crime,
I, Micca the partisan, haven't lain here many years,
Hadn't lived many more when darkness struck.

Passer-by, I ask no pardon of you or any other,
No prayer or lament, no special remembrance.
Only one thing I beg: that this peace of mine endure,
That heat and cold succeed each other endlessly above me,
Without fresh blood filtering through clods
To reach me with its deadly warmth,
Waking to new pain these bones long turned to stone.

6 October 1952
translated by Ruth Feldman

[259]

LEOPOLD STAFF
Three Towns

Three small towns,
So small that all of them
Could be contained in one . . .

They are not on the map.
They were destroyed in the war,
For in them lived people
Who were hard-working, quiet,
Peace-loving.

O tepid, indifferent brothers!
Why does none of you look for those towns?
How poor is the man who
asks no questions.

translated by Czesław Miłosz

GÜNTER KUNERT
On the Archaeology of Our Being Buried Alive

Rain, and rain again,
war, and war again
one merciful, one merciless
once, nature at first hand, once
at second hand.

A train runs again
after thirty years of fighting
on the same old line as before,
ruins disappear
but with them, the world
as it had been.

We never really take leave
of our past

because before we come to it
it collapsed
into dust and ashes, somewhere,
when it was still called present.

We would also like to embrace
the dead some time, if they had not been
made into words,
long skeins of words,
which no longer resemble a shape.

Had we been able to keep the voices
of dying, our ears would hardly
be so deafened from talk.
Sometimes things are
impenetrable, sometimes crystal clear
but like pieces of broken glass
before you cut yourself on them
and bleed to death.

translated by Trude Schwab and Desmond Graham

LILY BRETT

I Keep Forgetting

I keep forgetting
the facts and statistics
and each time
I need to know them

I look up books
these books line
twelve shelves
in my room

I know where to go
to confirm the fact
that in the Warsaw Ghetto
there were 7.2 people per room

and in Lodz
they allocated
5.8 people
to each room

I forget
over and over again
that one third of Warsaw
was Jewish

and in the ghetto
they crammed 500,000 Jews
into 2.4 per cent
of the area of the city

and how many
bodies were they burning
in Auschwitz
at the peak of their production

twelve thousand a day
I have to check
and re-check

and did I dream
that at 4pm on the 19th January
58,000 emaciated inmates
were marched out of Auschwitz

was I right
to remember that in Bergen Belsen
from the 4th-13th of April 1945
28,000 Jews arrived from other camps

I can remember
hundreds and hundreds
of phone numbers

phone numbers
I haven't phoned
for twenty years
are readily accessible

and I can remember
people's conversations
and what someone's wife
said to someone else's husband

what a good memory
you have
people tell me.

JAMES K. BAXTER

from *Elegy for an Unknown Soldier*

There was a time when I would magnify
His ending: scatter words as if I wept
Tears not of my own but man's; there was a time.
But not now so. He died of a common sickness.

Awkward at school, he could not master sums.
Could you expect him then to understand
The miracle and menace of his body
That grew as mushrooms grow from dusk to dawn?

He had the weight, though, for a football scrum,
And thought it fine to listen to the cheering
And drink beer with the boys, telling them tall
Stories of girls he had never known.

But when the War came he was glad and sorry,
But soon enlisted. Then his mother cried
A little, and his father boasted how
He'd let him go, though needed for the farm.

Likely in Egypt he would find out something
About himself, if flies and drunkenness
And deadly heat could tell him much—until
In his first battle a shell splinter caught him.

So crown him with memorial bronze among
The older dead, child of a mountainous island.

Who born of silence has burned back to silence.

OTTÓ ORBÁN

The Beauty of War

War's for the conquerors, for Alexander the Great,
the scoutmaster gazing with pleasure on his warriors warming
each other, stuck in life's freezer at that jamboree in Macedon.
They share their last fag, he brags to the Chronicle
though he heartily despises the liberal press
because they create such a stink at each piffling court-martial,
when even a blind man can see that civilization's at stake . . .
What's done is done, always look on the bright side!
Alas, the barbed wire has a circular section, all sides are bright;
war is the thing that Pilinsky saw, at the age of twenty-four;
time spinning according to the law of the camera
a frozen frame from an accelerated film of mad alternatives,
a cage that preserves the glow of damnation, the smoke and the heat;
the victims like poultry waiting for slaughter, struggling on the wire.

translated by George Szirtes

OTTO ORBAN

Gaiety and Good Heart

On this heavenly molehill
where a long-drawn-out war is being waged besides the local
          massacres
and the anonymous heroes of time squatting in the dug-outs of their
          days
know that a smile is only self-deception and joy is death's moratorium

for major causes are composed of minor causes
for victory is unreal in a battle where
peasants' huts are bombed with figures
for the business of living is a master sculptor and can twist a man's
      face to a sheep's
and in hunger there is neither poetry nor sense of the fundamentals
on this earth where poverty is no news
and no one is fool enough to stammer or cry in deep emotion
for who has not clambered down from some cross or other
and who has not soaked his nail-stuck feet in a bowl of water
what typist has not sprung to life again after her family was sent to
      the ovens
and who has not forgotten her unforgettable lover's features
where everybody but everybody has shaken hands with the bereaved
      widow
assuring her of his sympathy gazing deep into her eyes
and has cabled ALL THE BEST on hearing of the resurrection of
      Lazarus
where the idea of endurance was invented to meet the torture-chamber
where there is no one who has not seen it all
and who does not have endless opportunities
and who would gladly not exchange state affairs for a fishing-rod
on the breast of this barren mother
when the stars of cosmic paralysis transfix you to the dust
and you lean on the rail and look down into the valley
you can see the hope of the age the little rickety truck
stuffed with whatever has been salvaged from the fire
sticks of furniture sacks stewpans chickens
like an unkillable bombardier-beetle
like a tin-jowled reptile flashing headlamp-eyes
and lolling out its panting petrol-tongue like a child
while in front of the flames embossed on its jolting flanks
the nickel trade-mark shines:
Gaiety and Good Heart

translated by Edwin Morgan

ÁGNES GERGELY

With Lamp in Hand

Men! In exchange for a good piece
Of rib, you carve, you sculpt
From our bones—you have reigned
From the saddle,
Have beaten the anvil
For centuries,

Fiddling with slide-rules.
In your alembics what haven't you boiled
And distilled
Searching for treasures,
Walking the glinting stars
Or doggedly whetting stone knives.
At last beside
Shepherd waters you've contrived
Industry: in spring
When the seeds sprout
You clip, you kill;

For you the whole
World is mould.
You hang on our loins
Aprons
Or clothe us
In your abstractions—

O, you cry with bared chest,
I'm a hero! And we,
We manage somehow
To behold you. See,
After you fall
We see, we bandage your brow—

Last night my dream beheld me
Clothed in the white apron

Of Florence Nightingale
And you, you were wounded, shot in the lung
Or was it your legs that were maimed?
Beethoven-deaf, you
In that field hospital in the Crimea

And so mercifully, with the solace
Of febrifuge from ward to ward
I went with lamp in hand
And from the first breath I knew
That you'll start it all over again
And do wonders
Anew and silly things too,
My brothers.

translated by Daniel Hoffman

ZBIGNIEW HERBERT

Photograph

With this boy motionless as an Eleatic arrow
a boy among tall grass I have nothing in common
oavo a date of birth a papillary line

this photograph was taken by my father before the second Persian
        war
from the foliage and clouds I deduce August
songs of birds crickets the smell of crops abundance

below the river called on Roman maps Hipanis
a watershed approaching thunder advising shelter with the Greeks
their sea colonies were not so far away

the boy smiles trustingly the only shadow he knows
is a straw hat a pine house
the only glow sunset

my little Isaac bend your head
just a moment of pain and you shall be
whatever you desire – a swallow a wild lily

I must shed your blood my little one
for you to remain innocent in the summer lightning
safe for ever as an insect enclosed in amber
beautiful as a cathedral of fern preserved in coal

translated by Michael March

PRIMO LEVI

The Girl-Child of Pompeii

Since everyone's anguish is our own,
We live yours over again, thin child,
Clutching your mother convulsively
As though, when the noon sky turned black,
You wanted to re-enter her.
To no avail, because the air, turned poison,
Filtered to find you through the closed windows
Of your quiet thick-walled house,
Once happy with your song, your timid laugh.
Centuries have passed, the ash has petrified
To imprison those delicate limbs for ever.
In this way you stay with us, a twisted plaster cast,
Agony without end, terrible witness to how much
Our proud seed matters to the gods.
Nothing is left of your far-removed sister,
The Dutch girl imprisoned by four walls
Who wrote of her youth without tomorrows.
Her silent ash was scattered by the wind,
Her brief life shut into a crumpled notebook.
Nothing remains of the Hiroshima schoolgirl,
A shadow printed on a wall by the light of a thousand suns,
Victim sacrificed on the altar of fear.
Powerful of the earth, masters of new poisons,
Sad secret guardians of final thunder,

The torments heaven sends us are enough.
Before your finger presses down, stop and consider.

20 November 1978
translated by Ruth Feldman

INGEBORG BACHMANN

Every Day

War is no longer declared,
but continued. The outrageous
has become everyday. The hero
stays away from the battlefield. The weak
have advanced into the firing line.
The uniform of the day is patience,
the medal, the shabby star
of hope above the heart.

It is awarded
when the action is over
when the drumfire fades,
when the enemy is no longer in sight
but the shadow of everlasting weaponry
covers the sky.

It is awarded
for desertion,
for bravery in the face of friendship,
for the betrayal of disgraceful secrets
and disobedience
to any order.

translated by Trude Schwab and Desmond Graham

ACKNOWLEDGMENTS

Angel Books: Osip Mandelshtam, from *Selected Poems* (1991), trans. James Greene. Anvil Press Poetry: F.T. Prince, from *Collected Poems* (1979); Odysseus Elytis, from *Selected Poems* (1981), trans. © Edmund Keeley & Peter Sherrard 1981; George Seferis, from *Collected Poems* (1982), trans. © Edmund Keeley & Peter Sherrard 1982; Sándor Weöres, from *Eternal Moment: Selected Poems* (1988), trans. © Edwin Morgan 1982; János Pilinsky, from *Selected Poems* (1976). Louis Aragon: from *Aragon: Poet of Resurgent France* (Pilot Press, 1946). Avon Books: Rachel Korn, 'Sometimes I Want to Go Up' from *Voices Within the Ark* (1980), © Rachel Korn 1980; Chaim Grade, from ibid., trans. Marc Kaminsky; Amir Gilboa, from ibid., trans. A.C. Jacobs; Abba Kovner, from ibid.; Stanislaw Wygodski, from ibid. Ingeborg Bachmann: 'Every Day', trans. © Trude Schwab and Desmond Graham. Barrie & Jenkins: Ruth Pitter, from *End of Drought* (1975). Beacon Press: Miguel Hernandez, from *Selected Poems*. Bloodaxe Books Ltd.: Miroslav Holub, from *Poems Before and After: Collected English Translations* (1990), © Miroslav Holub 1990; Anna Akhmatova, from *Selected Poems* (1989). The Calder Educational Trust, London and the Erich Fried Estate: Erich Fried, from *One Hundred Poems Without A Country* (1978), trans. Stuart Hood, © Erich Fried 1978 and © this translation Stuart Hood 1979. Canongate Press PLC: William Montgomerie, from *Time to Time: Selected Poems* (1985), © William Montgomerie 1985. Carcanet Press Ltd.: HD from *Trilogy* (1983); Edwin Morgan extract from 'The New Divan' from *Collected Poems*; Edmund Blunden, from *Selected Poems* (1982). John Ciardi: from *39 Poems*, © John Ciardi 1959. Columbia University Press: Gyula Illyés, from *Modern Hungarian Poetry* (1977), trans. © William Jay Smith 1977; Ágnes Gergely, 'Crazed Man in a Concentration Camp' from ibid., trans. © Edwin Morgan 1977, 'Sign on My Door Jamb', trans. Thomas Land, 'With Lamp in Hand', trans. Daniel Hoffman; Imre Csanádi, from ibid., trans © Edwin Morgan 1977; Zoltan Zelk, trans. Daniel Hoffman; Ottó Orbán, 'The Beauty of War', trans. George Szirtes, 'With Gaiety & Good Heart', trans. Edwin Morgan. Corvina Press: Ágnes Nemes Nagy, from *Between: Selected Poems* (1988), trans. Hugh Maxton; Sándor Csoóri, from *Barbarian Prayer: Selected Poems* (1989); István Vas, from *Through the Smoke: Selected Poems* (1989), trans. William Jay Smith. R.N. Currey: 'Unseen Fire'. Andre Deutsch: Johannes Bobrowski, from *Selected Poems of Johannes Bobrowski and Horst Blener* (1971), trans. Ruth & Matthew Mead; Tadeusz Różewicz, from *Selected Poems*, trans. Adam Czerniawski, 1976. James Dickey: from *Poems 1957–1967* (Rapp & Carroll, 1967). Doubleday Inc.: Czesław Miłosz, from *Polish Post War Poetry* (1970), trans. Czesław Miłosz & Leopald Staff. Günter Eich: from *Valuable Nail*, © Günter Eich 1981. Faber & Faber Ltd: Allen Tate, from *Collected Poems 1919–1976*, © 1952, 1953, 1970, 1977 by Allen Tate; Randall Jarrell, from *Randall Jarrell: The Complete Poems*, © 1945, 1969 by Mrs Randall Jarrell, © renewed 1973 by Mrs Randall Jarrell; Richard Wilbur, from *Poems 1943–56* (Faber) © 1947 renewed © 1975 by Richard Wilbur; Wallace Stevens, from *Collected Poems*, © Wallace Stevens 1955; Edwin Muir, from *Collected Poems 1921–51*, © Edwin Muir 1952; W.H. Auden, from *W.H. Auden: Collected Poems*, ed. Edward Mendelson; Stephen Spender, from *Collected Poems 1928–53* (1955); Primo Levi, from *Collected Poems* (1988), trans. © Ruth Feldman & Brian Swann 1988. Flambard Press: Anna Kamienska, from *Two Darknesses* (1994), trans. © Tomasz P. Krzeszowski & Desmond Graham 1994. Forest Books: Ioan Alexandru, from *An Anthology of Contemporary Romanian Poetry* (1984), trans. Andrea Deletant & Brenda Walker. John Fuller: Roy Fuller, from *Collected Poems* (Deutsch, 1962), © The Estate of Roy Fuller. Robert Garioch: from *Collected Poems* (Macdonald, 1977). Rupert Glover: Dennis Glover, from *The Wind and the Sound* (1945). Michael Hamburger: Paul Celan, from *Selected Poems* (Anvil, 1988), trans. © Michael Hamburger 1988; Peter Huchel, from *Selected Poems* (Carcanet, 1974) trans. © Michael Hamburger 1974; Günter Grass, from *Selected Poems*, trans. © Michael Hamburger 1969. Hamish Henderson: from *Elegies for the Dead in Cyrenaica* (E.U.S.P.B., Edinburgh, 1977). HarperCollins Publishers Australia: John Quinn, from *Battle Stations*; David Campbell, from *Collected Poems*; Eric Rolls, from *Selected Poems*; Kenneth Slessor, from *Selected Poems*; Judith Wright, from *Collected Poems*; Douglas Stewart, from *Sonnets to the Unknown Soldier*. Harper-Collins Publishers Ltd.: Alun Lewis, from *Selected Poems* (George Allen & Unwin, 1981); Angelos Sikelianos, from *Selected Poems* (George Allen & Unwin 1979) trans. © Edmund Keeley & Peter Sherrard 1979. David Higham Associates Ltd.: Charles Causley, 'Recruiting Drive' from *Collected Poems* and 'Song of the Dying Gunner' from *Farewell Aggie Weston* (Macmillan); Louis MacNeice, from *Selected Poems* (Faber, 1964); Edith Sitwell, from *The Song of the Cold* (Macmillan, 1945); Dylan Thomas from *The Poems* (J.M. Dent). Holocaust Publications Inc.: Luba Krugman Gurdus, from *Painful Echoes: Poems of the Holocaust*; Charles Reznikoff, 'The Letter' from ibid. Geoffrey Holloway: from *Rhine Jump* (1974), © Geoffrey Holloway 1974. Pierre Jean-Jouve: from *An Idiom of Night*. Jewish Publishing Society: poems by two children from Terezin from *Anthology of Holocaust Literature* (1969), ed. Jacob Glatstein, Israel Knox & Samuel Magoshes. Günter Kunert: 'On the Archaeology of Our Being Buried Alive'. Macdonald: Robert Garioch, from *Collected Poems* (1977). James MacGibbon, as literary executor: Stevie Smith, from *Collected Poems*. Sorley MacLean: 'Heroes', 'Going Westwards', from *Collected Poems*. Melbourne University Press: Lily Brett, from *After the War*; C.D. Griffin from *Clubbing of the Gunfire: 101 Australian War Poems* (1984). Menard Press: Rudolf Langer, from *Wounded No Doubt*, trans. Ewald Osers (1979); Jerzy Ficowski, from *A Reading of Ashes*, trans. Keith Bosley & Krystyna Wandycz. Methuen London: Bertolt Brecht, 'Great Babel Gives Birth', trans. John Willett, 'The God of War', trans. Michael Hamburger, '1940', trans. Sammy McLean from *Poems 1913–1956*. Stephen Mitchell: Dan Pagis, from *Poems* (1972), trans. © Stephen Mitchell 1972. Edwin Morgan: Salvatore Quasimodo, 'The Soldiers Cry at Night', 'Man of My Time', 'Snow', all trans. Edwin Morgan. Mosaic Press: Rachel Korn, 'Arthur Ziegelboim', 'Lot's Wife', 'My Mother Often Wept' from *Generations* (1982), trans. Ruth Whitman. Mrs M. Nemerov: Howard Nemerov, from *Collected Poems* (1977), © The Estate of Howard Nemerov. Northern House: Sorley Maclean, from *Poems to Eimhir*. Oberon Press: Raymond Souster, from *So Far So Good* (1969). Open University Press: Sankichi Toge, from *Modern Japanese Poetry* (1979). Peter Owen Ltd.: Eugen Jebeleanu, from *Anthology of Contemporary Romanian Poetry* (1969). Oxford University Press: Bernard Spencer, from *Bernard Spencer: Collected Poems*, © Mrs Anne Humphreys 1981; Keith Douglas, from *The Complete Poems of Keith Douglas*, © Marie J. Douglas 1978; Zbigniew Herbert, from *Zbigniew Herbert: Selected Poems*, trans. John Carpenter & Bogdana Carpenter, © John Carpenter & Bogdana Carpenter 1971; Henry Reed, from *Collected Poems*, © OUP 1991; Marina Tsvetayeva, from *Selected Poems*, trans. Elaine Feinstein; James Baxter, from *The Rock Woman* (1967). Penguin Books Ltd.: Kaoru Maruyama, Tamiki Hara & Jun Okamoto, from *The Penguin Book of Japanese Poetry* (1964), trans. © Geoffrey Bownas & Anthony Thwaite; Leopold

BIOGRAPHICAL NOTES

The notes offer information relevant to the field of this anthology. A reference for further reading is given for each poet. A name in italics at the end of an entry refers to an anthology listed after these Notes.

Akhmatova, Anna (1889–1966); b. St Petersburg, evacuated to Tashkent from Leningrad (1941–4); 'Courage' pub. in *Pravda* in 1942; trans. in *Selected Poems* (1989)

Alexandru, Ioan (b. 1941); Romanian; trans. in *Deletant*

Allison, Drummond (1921–44); b. Caterham; served in N. Africa; killed in Italy; *The Yellow Night* (1945)

Aragon, Louis (b. 1897); served against the Germans in the early part of the war; trans. in *Aragon: Poet of the Resistance* (1946)

Auden, W. H. (1907–73); b. York; wrote extensively on the 1930s; emigrated to USA 1938; *Collected Poems* (1976)

Ayukawa, Nobuo (1920–1985); b. Tokyo; served in armed forces during the war; trans. in *Guest*

Bachmann, Ingeborg (1926–73); b. Klagenfurth; pub. 1953, later renounced poetry for prose fiction; trans. *In the Storm of Roses* (1986)

Baczyński, Krzysztof Kamil (1921–44); was killed in the Warsaw uprising; no collected translation

Baxter, James K. (1926–72); b. Dunedin, NZ; *Collected Poems* (1979)

Birney, Earle (b. 1904 in Calgary); served in Canadian Army overseas as a personnel selection officer; *Ghost in the Wheels: Selected Poems* (1977)

Bishop, Elizabeth (1911–79); b. New England; *Complete Poems 1927–1979* (1984)

Blunden, Edmund (1896–1974); b. London; important poet and autobiographer of the First World War; *Shells by a Stream* (1944)

Bobrowski, Johannes (1917–65); b. Tilsit; served in German Army on Eastern front and began writing then; also novelist and short story writer of war; trans. in *Penguin Modern European Poets* series (1971)

Brecht, Bertolt (1891–1956); b. Augsburg; fled Nazi Germany 1933, moving just ahead of advancing armies and then to America; trans. *Poems* (1976)

Brett, Lily (b. 1946 in Germany); came to Melbourne 1948; also novelist of the Holocaust; *After the War* (1990)

Campbell, David (1915–79); b. Ellerslie Station, NSW; pilot and squadron commander in RAAF; *Selected Poems* (1973)

Causley, Charles (b. 1917 in Launceston, Cornwall); served in Royal Navy 1940–46; *Farewell Aggie Weston* (1951)

Celan, Paul [Paul Antschel] (1920–70); b. Czernowitz, Bukovina; parents deported by the Nazis; committed suicide; trans. *Selected Poems* (1988)

Char, René (b. 1907); leading Resistance fighter in Provence; trans. *Poems* (1959)

Ciardi, John (b. 1916, Boston, MA); served in US Army Air Corps; *39 Poems* (1959); also a war diary, *Saipan* (1988)

Csnádi, Imre (b. 1920 in western Hungary); conscripted; PoW in Ukraine; trans. in *Vajda*

Csoóri, Sándor (b. 1930 in western Hungary); trans. *Barbarian Prayer* (1989)

Currey, R. N. (b. 1907 in S. Africa); joined the army 1941, posted to

India 1943; *This Other Planet* (1945); also *Poets of the 1939–45 War* (1960)

Dickey, James (b. 1923 in Atlanta, Georgia); US Air Force; *Poems 1957–1967* (1967)

Douglas, Keith (1920–44); b. Tunbridge Wells; tank commander in N. Africa; war narrative *Alamein to Zem Zem* (1946); *Complete Poems* (1978)

Eberhart, Richard (b. 1904 in Austin, Minnesota); served as aerial gunnery instructor in US Navy; *Collected Poems* (1960)

Eich, Günter (1907–72); in German army 1939–45; Hans Magnus Enzensburger wrote of 'Inventory' that it was 'regarded as the birth certificate of the new German poetry'; trans. *Valuable Nail* (1981)

Elytis, Odysseus (b. 1911 in Crete); lived in Athens; served in the Greek army on the Albanian Front in the Greek-Italian war; the 'Song' first pub. 1945; Nobel Prize 1979; *Selected Poems* (1981)

Ficowski, Jerzy (b. 1924); served in the Polish Army at the start of the war; trans. *A Reading of Ashes* (1981)

Fried, Erich (1921–1988); b. Vienna; emigrated to London 1938; *One Hundred Poems Without a Country* (1978)

Fuller, Roy (1919–90); b. Failsworth; in Royal Navy; wrote and published widely during the war; *Collected Poems 1934–1984* (1985)

Garioch, Robert (1909–81); b. Edinburgh; served in war; *Collected Poems* (1977)

Gebirtig, Mordecai (1877–1942); b. Cracow; popular balladist; killed in Crakow Ghetto; 'Our Town is Burning' became one of the most popular songs in the Ghettos and Concentration Camps; in *Glatstein*

Gergely, Ágnes (b. 1933 in Budapest); also a novelist; in *Vajda*

Gilboa, Amir (b. 1917 in Poland); emigrated to 'Palestine' 1937; served

[277]

in British Army during the war, publishing from 1942; trans. (from Hebrew) in *Schwartz*

Glover, Denis (1912–80); b. Dunedin; served in NZ division of the RN in the Arctic and the Normandy Landings; narrative *Hot Water Sailor* (1962); *The Wind and the Sand* (1945)

Grade, Chaim (b. 1910, Vilna); a refugee in Russia during the war; after the war returned to Vilna; emigrated to U.S.; also a novelist; trans. (from Yiddish) in *Schwartz*

Grass, Günter (b. 1927, Danzig [Gdańsk]); conscription at sixteen, wounded in 1945; also novelist of the war; trans. *Selected Poems* (1966)

Griffin, C. D. (Sir David) (b. 1915 in Sydney); served in Australian Imperial Force from 1940; prisoner of the Japanese in Changi 1942–5; in *Wallace-Crabbe*

Gurdus, Luba Krugman (b. 1914 in Bialystok); started writing (in Polish) in the Ghetto, April 1943; her son Bobus died of diphtheria aged 4; the poems are from her diary of the time; also memoirs, *The Death Train* (1978); trans. *Painful Echoes: Poems of the Holocaust* (1985)

Hampson, Norman (b. 1922); in Royal Navy; war poems in numerous periodicals; in *Hamilton*

Hara, Tamiki (1905–51); survived Hiroshima; committed suicide after confirmation of symptoms of 'atom disease'; also, *Summer Flowers*, a novel on Hiroshima; trans. in *Guest*

HD (1886–1961); b. Bethlehem, Pennsylvania; lived in London during the Blitz; *The Walls Do Not Fall* (1944)

Henderson, Hamish (b. 1919 in Perthshire); in 51st Highland Division; *Elegies for the Dead in Cyrenaica* (1948)

Herbert, Zbigniew (b. 1924 in Lvov); fought in Polish Resistance; not published till after Stalin's death; widely trans.; trans. in *Selected Poems* (1977)

Hernandez, Miguel (1910–42); b. Alicante; fought in Spanish Civil War; died of TB after three years in Franco's prisons; 'War' written in prison *c.* 1939; 'Onion Lullaby' one of his last poems from prison, *c.* 1942; *Selected Poems* (1972)

Holan, Vladimír (1905–80); b. Prague; published poems in the 1930s and after; trans. in *Penguin Modern European Poets* series (1971)

Holloway, Geoffrey (b. 1918 in Birmingham); served in RAMC 1939–46; *Rhine Jump* (1974)

Holub, Miroslav (b. 1923 in Pilsen); widely trans. from the Czech; also immunologist and researcher; in *Poems Before and After* (1990)

Huchel, Peter (1903–81); b. Berlin; military service 1940–45; soldier on the Eastern Front; trans. *The Garden of Theophrastus* (1983)

Iijima, Koichi (b. 1930); trans. in *Guest*

Illyés, Gyula (1902–83); b. western Hungary; widely trans.; *Selected Poems* (1971)

Jarrell, Randall (1914–65); b. Nashville, Tennessee; briefly served as pilot then as instructor, USAF; *Complete Poems* (1971)

Jean-Jouve, Pierre (b. 1897); in Switzerland during the war; trans. *An Idiom of Night* (1968)

Jebeleanu, Eugen (b. 1911); Romanian; trans. in *Hastie*

Kamieńska, Anna (1920–86); b. Krasnystaw, eastern Poland; taught in Underground schools in Lublin area; trans. *Two Darknesses* (1994)

Kaminsky, Marc (b. 1943); 'Carrying My Brother' follows testimony in *Death in Life: Survivors of Hiroshima* (1967); 'Every Month' follows testimony of Sachiko Habu in *Children of the A Bomb: The Testament of Boys and Girls in Hiroshima* (1982); *The Road from Hiroshima* (1984)

Kaneko, Mitsuharu (1895–1975); widely travelled before the war; the only major Japanese poet to write anti-war poems during the war, most of them published in 1948; trans. in *Bownas*

Kocbek, Edvard (1904–81); b. Slovenia; partisan during the war; trans. in *Weissbort 1991*

Korn, Rachel (1898–1982); b. Galicia; lived in Lvov until 1941; fled to Soviet Union and emigrated to Canada; trans. (from Yiddish) *Paper Roses* (1985)

Kovner, Abba (b. 1918 in Sebastopol); settled in Vilna; hid with nuns; a commander in the Vilna Ghetto and afterwards a partisan; embarked for Palestine 1945; publishing (in Hebrew) since 1947; *My Little Sister* (trans. 1986) written to an imaginary sister; trans. in *Penguin Modern European Poets* series (1971)

Kunert, Günter (b. 1929 in Berlin); found unfit to serve in the army through his part Jewish descent; after the war writing in East and then West Germany; trans. in *Hamburger*

Langer, Rudolf (b. 1923 in Silesia); from 1943 lived in Germany; trans. *Wounded No Doubt and Pale From Battle* (1979)

Levi, Primo (1919–87); b. Turin; survived Auschwitz; also prose fiction from his Camp experience; a chemist; *Collected Poems* (1992)

Lewis, Alun (1915–44); b. Aberdare, S. Wales; army; died under mysterious circumstances in Burma before seeing action; also short stories of war; *Selected Poems* (1981)

MacLean, Sorley (b. 1911 on island of Raasay); wounded at El Alamein; writes in Gaelic; trans. in *Spring Tide and Neap Tide* (1976)

MacNeice, Louis (1907–63); b. Belfast; writing from the 1930s and a lot in wartime; *Collected Poems* (1966)

Mandelshtam, Osip (1891–1938); b. Warsaw; moved to St Petersburg, main figure among poets there; arrested in 1934 then in camps and 'exile'; died in Siberia; widely trans.; in *Penguin Modern European Poets* series (1977)

Maruyama, Kaoru (1899–1974); b. Oita Prefecture; trans. in *Bownas*

Miłosz, Czesław (b. 1911 in Lithuania); edited Underground publications in occupied Warsaw; Nobel Prize 1980; in *Milosz*

Montale, Eugenio (1896–1982); in 1938 resigned a curator's post rather than work with the Fascists; spent war in Florence, but published in Switzerland; Nobel Prize 1975; in *Penguin Modern European Poets* series (1969)

Montgomerie, William (1904–1994); *From Time to Time* (1985)

Morgan, Edwin (b. 1920 in Glasgow); served in RAMC; *The New Divan* (1977)

Muir, Edwin (1887–1959); b. Orkney and moved to Glasgow; *Collected Poems* (1960)

Nagy, Ágnes Nemes (b. 1922 in Budapest); trans. *Between: Selected Poems* (1988)

Nemerov, Howard (1920–91); b. New York; served in Royal Canadian AF and US Army Air Corps (attached to RAF) 1941–5; *Collected Poems* (1977)

Okamoto, Jun (b. 1901); communist and editor; trans. in *Bownas*

Orbán, Ottó (b. 1936 in Budapest); father killed in a Concentration Camp; brought up in School for War Orphans; trans. in *Vajda*

Pagis, Dan (1930–86); b. Bukovina into Germanized Jewish home; early adolescence in a Concentration Camp; trans. (from Hebrew) *Selected Poems* (1972)

Pasternak, Boris (1890–1960); b. Moscow; *Dr Zhivago* and award of Nobel Prize; *Selected Poems* (1959)

Pilinsky, János (1921–81); b. Budapest; military service from 1944; during war spent months in Prisoner of War Camps; trans. *Selected Poems* (1976)

Pitter, Ruth (1897–1992); b. Ilford; *Collected Poems* (1968)

Prince, F. T. (b. 1912 in Kimberley, S. Africa); served in N. Africa; *Collected Poems* (1979)

Quasimodo, Salvatore (1901–68); Sicilian; in Milan during the war; Nobel Prize 1959; trans. in *Collected Poems* (1983)

Quinn, John (b. 1915 in Canada; moved to Australia); served in Australian Imperial Force in Middle East and New Guinea; *Battle Stations* (1944)

Radnóti, Miklós (1909–44); b. Budapest; well established Hungarian poet before the war; from 1940, as a Jew, in various Forced Labour Battalions constructing railway line Bor-Belgrade; evacuated, shot on forced march; when exhumed in 1945, a notebook full of poems was found in his raincoat; trans. *Forced March: Selected Poems* (1979)

Reed, Henry (1914–86); b. Birmingham; called up in 1941; released following year to work in Foreign Office; *Collected Poems* (1991)

Reznikoff, Charles (b. 1894); American; *Holocaust* (1975); also *The Complete Poems* (1977)

Rolls, Eric (b. 1923, in Grenfell, NSW); served as 18-year-old signaller in Papua New Guinea; *Selected Poems* (1990)

Ross, Alan (b. 1922); served in Royal Navy; *Open Sea* (1975)

Różewicz, Tadeusz (b. 1921 in Radmosko); in the Polish Underground during the war; widely trans.; trans. in *Penguin Modern European Poets* series (1976)

Sachs, Nelly (1891–1970); b. Berlin; publishing in 1920s; emigrated to Sweden 1940; joint Nobel Prize 1966; trans. *O The Chimneys* (1961); *Selected Poems* (1968)

Saga, Nobuyuki; (b. 1902 in Miyazaki Prefecture) trans. in *Kajima*

Scannell, Vernon (b. 1922); served in the Middle East and Europe; also criticism, *Poets of the Second World War*; *Soldiering On* (1989)

Scovell, E. J. (b. 1907 in Sheffield); lived in Oxford during the war; *Shadows of Chrysanthemums* (1944); also in *Reilly*

Seferis, George (1900–71); Greek; in Alexandria during the war; Nobel Prize 1963; trans. in *Collected Poems* (1982)

Seifert, Jaroslav (b. 1901); in Prague during the war; widely trans.; Nobel Prize 1984; trans. in *Selected Poems* (1986)

Sikelianos, Angelos (1884–1951); 'Agaraphon' was written during the Occupation of Greece, autumn 1941; trans. in *Selected Poems* (1979)

Simpson, Louis (b. 1923 in Jamaica); enlisted US Army 1943; glider Infantry Regiment; served in Europe; after surviving the war had a nervous breakdown which brought amnesia; in these conditions started writing poems; also autobiography, *Air with Armed Men* (1972); *Selected Poems* (1966)

Sitwell, Edith (1887–1964); 'Still Falls The Rain', her most famous poem from the Blitz; *The Song of the Cold* (1945)

Slessor, Kenneth (1901–71); b. Orange, NSW; 1940–44 Australian Official War Correspondent, covering overseas campaigns; *Poems* (1957)

Slutsky, Boris (b. 1919 in Ukraine); served in the Russian Army 1941–5; trans. in *Weissbort*

Smith, Stevie (1902–71); b. Hull; moved to London; also novelist of war period; *Collected Poems* (1975)

Souster, Raymond (b. 1921 in Toronto); served in RCAF in Canada and at the war's end in Europe; *So Far So Good* (1969)

Spencer, Bernard (1909–63); b. Madras; travelled widely with British Council; civilian in Alexandria during the war; *Collected Poems* (1981)

Spender, Stephen (b. 1909); served in Fire Service in London; established during 1930s and writing much of the war; *Collected Poems* (1954)

Staff, Leopold (1878–1957); b. Lvov; first pub. 1901; trans. in *Miłosz*

Stevens, Wallace (1879–1955); b. Reading, Pennsylvania; first pub. 1923; poems relating to both First and Second Wars; *Collected Poems* (1955)

Stewart, Douglas (1918–85); b. Eltham, NZ; in Australia from 1938; *Sonnets to the Unknown Soldier* (1941)

Sutzkever, Abraham (b. 1913 near Vilna); wrote poems in Vilna Ghetto and as partisan; escaped to Moscow; testified at the Nuremburg Trials; trans. in *Howe* and *Burnt Pearls: Ghetto Poems* (1981)

Świrszczyńska, Anna [Anna Swir] (1909–84); b. Warsaw; in the literary Underground during Occupation; trans. *Building the Barricade* (1979)

Tate, Allen (1899–1979); b. Kentucky; *Poems 1922–1947*

Thomas, Dylan (1914–53); b. Swansea; worked on documentary films in London during war; *Collected Poems 1934–1953* (1988)

Toge, Sankichi (1917–1953); b. Usaka; lived in Hiroshima; known in Japan as a poet of the Atom Bomb; died from the effects of radiation; trans. in *Davis*

Tsvetayeva, Marina (1892–1941); b. Moscow; established early reputation as a poet; later life in exile, at first in Prague; trans. in *Selected Poems* (1981)

Tvardovsky, Alexander (1910–71); 'Tyorkin' an epic war poem with its 'Schweik'-like soldier was highly popular in the Soviet Union; trans. *Vasilli Tyorkin* (1975)

Two Children of Terezin; first published in *Children's Drawings and Poems (Terezin 1942–44)* (Prague 1959); in *Glatstein*

Vaptsarov, Nikola (1909–42); b. Bansko, Bulgaria; a Communist and Resistance organizer; tortured and shot; *Nineteen Poems* (1984)

Vas, István (b. 1910 in Budapest); of Jewish background, became a Catholic; during the war Forced Labour, attempted suicide then lived in hiding; 'Boccherini's Tomb' describes the school where he and his fellow Jews were kept; trans. *Through the Smoke* (1989)

Vinokurov, Evgeny (b. 1925); aged 17 in command of an artillery section; served on Ukrainian Front; trans. in *The War Is Over* (1976)

Warr, Bertram (1917–43); b. Toronto; joined RAF, killed in action; *In Quest of Beauty* (1950)

Weöres, Sándor (1913–89); b. western Hungary; a librarian during the war; trans. *Eternal Moment* (1988)

Wilbur, Richard (b. 1912 in New York); served in the US Infantry in France and Germany; *Poems 1943–56* (1957)

Woodcock, George (b. 1912 in Canada); editor of *Now* in London during the war; in *Atwood*

Woodruff, Donald M.; Canadian; poem taken from magazine *Contemporary Verse*; in *Birney*

Wright, Judith (b. 1915, near Armidale, NSW); in Europe when war broke out; returned to Australia to help with the property when her brothers enlisted; *Collected Poems* (1994)

Wygodski, Stanislaw [Stanislaw Gocki]; b. 1907 in Bedzin, Poland; deported to Auschwitz where he survived; emigrated to Israel in 1968; in *Schwartz*

Yamaguchi, Ei; not much is known about him; trans. in *Kôno*

Zelk, Zoltán (b. 1906 in Érmihályfalva [now in Romania]); son of a village Cantor, Forced Labour 1942–4; first published 1925; trans. in *Vajda*

ANTHOLOGIES

Atwood: The New Oxford Book of Canadian Verse in English (1982), chosen by Margaret Atwood

Birney: Twentieth Century Canadian Poetry (1953), ed. Earle Birney

Bownas: Penguin Book of Japanese Verse (1964), comp. Geoffrey Bownas and Anthony Thwaite

Davis: Modern Japanese Poetry (1979), trans. A. R. Davis

Deletant: An Anthology of Contemporary Romanian Poetry (1984), comp. Andrea Deletant and Brenda Walker

Glatstein: Anthology of Holocaust Literature (1969), ed. Jacob Glatstein

Guest: Post-War Japanese Poetry (1973), ed. Harry and Lynn Guest

Hamburger: East German Poetry (1972), ed. Michael Hamburger

Hamilton: The Poetry of War 1939–45 (1965), ed. Ian Hamilton

Hastie: Anthology of Contemporary Romanian Poetry (1969), comp. Roy MacGregor Hastie

Howe: Penguin Book of Yiddish Verse (1987) ed. Irving Howe

Kajima: The Poetry of Post-War Japan (1974), ed. Hajime Kajima

Kônô: An Anthology of Modern Japanese Poetry (1957), ed. Ichiro Kônô and Rikutaro Fukuda

Miłosz: Post-War Polish Poetry (1965; 3rd. ed. 1983), ed. Czesław Miłosz

Reilly: Chaos of the Night: Women's Poetry and Verse of the Second World War (1984), sel. Catherine Reilly

Schwartz: Voices Within the Ark: Modern Jewish Poets (1980), ed Howard Schwartz and Anthony Rudolf

Vajda: Modern Hungarian Poetry (1977), comp. Miklos Vajda

Wallace-Crabbe: Clubbing of the Gunfire: 101 Australian War Poems (1984), ed. Chris Wallace-Crabbe and Peter Pierce

Weissbort: Post-War Russian Poetry (1974), comp. Daniel Weissbort

Weissbort 1991: The Poetry of Survival: Post-War Poets of Central and Eastern Europe (1991), comp. Daniel Weissbort

INDEX OF POETS

INDEX OF TITLES AND FIRST LINES